917.292 Run

Runge, Jonathan.

Rum & Reggae's Jamaica

APR - 9

Rum & Reggae's
JAMAICA

by
Jonathan Runge

RUM & REGGAE GUIDEBOOKS, Inc. •
Prides Crossing, Massachusetts • 2002

While every effort has been made to provide accurate information, the prices, places, and people do change rather frequently in Jamaica. Typographical errors also occasionally occur. Thus, please keep in mind that there may be discrepancies between what you find and what is reported here. In addition, some of the recommendations have been given by individuals interviewed by the authors and may not represent the opinion of the author or of Rum & Reggae Guidebooks, Inc. The reader assumes all responsibility when participating in the activities or excursions described in this book.

Copyright © 2002 by Rum & Reggae Guidebooks, Inc.

All rights reserved under International and Pan-American Copyright Conventions. Published in the United States by Rum & Reggae Guidebooks, Inc., Boston, MA. All rights reserved. No part of this book may be used or reproduced in any manner whatsoever without written permission except in the case of brief quotations embodied in critical articles or reviews. For information, contact Rum & Reggae Guidebooks, Inc., P.O. Box 152, Prides Crossing, MA 01965

Rum & Reggae's Jamaica™ and Rum & Reggae™ are trademarks of Rum & Reggae Guidebooks, Inc.

ISBN: 1-893675-06-8
LIBRARY OF CONGRESS CATALOG CARD NUMBER: 2001119640

Book design by Scott-Martin Kosofsky and Betsy Sarles at The Philidor Company, Cambridge, MA

Cover design by Betsy Sarles & Jonathan Runge

Maps by Tony Lulek and Bruce Withey
Printed in Canada on recycled paper

For Nan

CONTENTS

Map . . . . viii–ix	
Preface xi	
Acknowledgments xiii	
Introduction xv	
Before You Go xvii	
Climate xvii	
Building a Base for Tanning xviii	
What to Wear and Take Along xviii	
Jamaica Superlatives xx	
The Ten Best Beaches in Jamaica xxi	
Lodging and Restaurant Key xxii	
Touristo Scale Key xxiv	
Rum & Reggae Punch . . . xxv	
Overview 1	
The Briefest History of a Complex Country 4	
Key Facts 6	
Getting There 6	
Getting Around 7	

Focus on Jamaica: Sex and Drugs and Reggae, Mon! . . . 8
   Negril—All your Brain and Body Needs 9
   Kingston—Rastaman Vibrations, Yeah (Positive) 11
   Reggae's Roots 12
   Reggae SumFest 14

Other Cool Jamaican Stuff . . 14
   Jamaican Art 14
   Greens-by-the-Sea— Montego Bay Golf 16

Where to Stay 18
   Negril 18
   Montego Bay 24
   Ochos Rios 29
   Port Antonio 31
   The South Coast 37
   Kingstown 38

Where to Eat 40
   Negril 40
   Montego Bay 42
   Port Antonio 42
   Kingstown 43

Don't Miss 45

Index 49

Write to Rum & Reggae 51

The Author 53

NEGRIL

0 — 1 MILE

- BLOODY BAY
- NEGRIL CABINS
- AIRPORT
- HEDONISM II
- COSMO'S RESTAURANT
- MARGARITAVILLE
- WHITE SANDS
- ROOTS BAMBOO
- RISKY BUSINESS
- ALFRED'S
- PETE'S RESTAURANT
- KUYABA
- DEBUSS
- TOURIST BOARD
- POST OFFICE
- ROUNDABOUT
- MISS BROWN'S
- MX III
- NEGRIL PLAZA
- PICKLED PARROT
- ROCKHOUSE
- TENSING PEN
- CATCH A FALLING STAR
- RICK'S CAFE
- THE CAVES
- LIGHTHOUSE

Surrounding area

- COYABA BEACH RESORT
- IRONSHORE
- HALF MOON
- RITZ-CARLTON ROSE HALL
- WYNDHAM ROSE
- SANGSTER AIRPORT
- NEGRIL BEACH
- LUCEA
- ROUND HILL
- MONTEGO BAY
- TRYALL
- SAVANNA-LA-MAR
- Y'S FALLS
- BLUEFIELDS
- JAKE'S

JAMAICA

DUNNE'S RIVER FALLS
OCHO RIOS
JAMAICA INN
NAVY ISLAND
TRIDENT VILLAS
SCOVERY BAY
FIREFLY
PORT ANTONIO
JAMAICA PALACE
ALMOUTH
RUNAWAY BAY
ANOTTO BAY
BUFF BAY
HOPE BAY
FRENCHMAN'S COVE
DRAGON BAY HOTEL
BLUE LAGOON (VILLAS)
BOSTON BAY
MOCKINGBIRD HILL
STRAWBERRY HILL
GOLBIN HILL
LONG BAY
MANDEVILLE
KINGSTON
MAY PEN
SPANISHTOWN
BLUE MT. PEAK (7402 FT.)
PORT ROYAL
MANLEY AIRPORT

0   10   20
MILES

N

PREFACE

RUM & REGGAE'S *Jamaica* is the fifth book to be published by Rum & Reggae Guidebooks, Inc. Writing these books is now a team effort. For *Rum & Reggae's Jamaica*, David Swanson was a contributor. Here's his bio:

David Swanson is a San Diego-based freelance writer who has been traveling to the Caribbean for the past 16 years. Although he enjoys all of the islands to varying degrees, he has particularly enjoyed discovering the region's more exotic corners, including Haiti, Cuba (in 1989, just as the Soviet Union was dropping aid), and the summit of Montserrat's smoldering volcano. Swanson's work has appeared in more than 45 North American newspapers and assorted magazines, including *Caribbean Travel and Life, American Way,* and *National Geographic Traveler, Caribbean, The Atlanta Journal-Constitution,* biztravel.com, *Bridal Guide, Chicago Magazine, Islands,* and numerous other publications.

We hope you enjoy the book. Please be sure to visit our Web site at www.rumreggae.com.

ACKNOWLEDGMENTS

CONTRARY TO WHAT YOU MIGHT THINK, writing a book on Jamaica is not very glamorous. The most glittering part about doing it is answering the "So what do you do?" question at cocktail parties. It's all uphill from there. We did not spend our days on the beach or by the pool sipping a rum punch. Well, okay, sometimes we did. But most of the time we were running around checking out this or that and complaining about the heat. Just when we started to get comfortable in a place, it was time to uproot ourselves and start all over again. Try doing that at least every other day and you'll begin to know what we mean.

Fortunately, some wonderful people helped us out along the way. We'd like to take this opportunity to sincerely thank those who did. In no particular order, they are Josef Forstmayr, Roland Alonzi, Marcella Martinez, Virginia Haynes, Gay Myers, and all those wonderful folks at the Jamaica Tourist Board and Peter Martins Associates. If we overlooked your name, sorry, but thanks for your help!

Rum & Reggae's Jamaica is published by Rum & Reggae Guidebooks, Inc. I have a lot of helpers and all deserve a hearty thanks. First and foremost, a lot of credit for this book goes to David Swanson, my chief Caribbean writer, editor, and general bon vivant of the West Coast. My warmest gratitude also goes to the following: our wonderful book designers, Betsy Sarles and Scott-Martin Kosofsky; our very talented web designer, Michael Carlson; our corporate illustrator and animation megastar, Eric Orner; our cartographers, Bruce Withey and Tony Lulek; our distributor, Midpoint Trade Books and its great staff, Gail Kump, Eric Kampf, Chris Bell and Julie Borgelt; our printer, Transcontinental Printing, and its terrific rep, Ed Catania; and our patient copy editor and indexer, Judith Antonelli.

There were several people who helped in other ways. Many thanks to Nan Garland, Duncan Donahue and Tom Fortier, Elvis Jiménez-Chávez and Chris Lawrence, Tom Jonsson, and Gedy Moody.

Finally, wicked thanks to our staff members, Joe Shapiro—the Director of Marketing and Sales and a Brasil nut; and Lauren White, copy editor, proofreader, and all-around great gal. Tons of thanks also to my business partner and right-hand man, Tony Lulek; and to my parents, Eunice and Albert Runge, for their continued enthusiasm and support.

And a can of dolphin-safe tuna to my cat and guardian angel, Jada.

To all who helped, many thanks—YAH MON!

Jonathan Runge
Author and Publisher
Rum & Reggae Guidebooks, Inc.
Prides Crossing, Massachusetts
March 1, 2002

INTRODUCTION

OUR MIDDLE NAME IS BITCH.™ That's how we describe our distinct point of view. *Rum & Reggae's Jamaica* is not your typical tourist guidebook to the birthplace of Bob Marley. We like to say that the Rum & Reggae series is written for people who want more out of a vacation than the standard tourist fare. Our reader is more sophisticated and independent. He's also more active—be it scuba diving, windsurfing, art hunting, hiking, sailing, golfing, playing tennis, exploring, or cocktailing. Or she's more particular, in search of places that are secluded, cerebral, spiritual, or très branché (if you have to ask what the latter means, those places are not for you).

This book differs from other guidebooks in another way. Instead of telling you that everything is "nice"—nice, that is, for the average Joe—*Rum & Reggae's Jamaica* offers definitive opinions. We will tell you what's fantastic and what's not, from the point of view of someone who loathes the tourist label and the other bland travel books whose names we won't mention.

We'll take you all over the island and share our recommendations of where to go (and where not to go). More importantly, we filter out all the crap for you so you can have fun reading the book and enjoy your vacation and keep the decision making to a minimum. We wish we had this book when we were doing our research. It would have made our job a helluva lot easier. We would have had more time to kick back and get sand between our toes.

So mix yourself a rum punch (we even provide the best recipe), put on some Bob Marley, and sit back and let *Rum & Reggae's Jamaica* take you on your own private voyage to feel all right.

BEFORE YOU GO

Climate

The weather in Jamaica is about as close to perfect as anywhere on Earth. The temperature rarely dips below 70 degrees or scales to above 90 degrees F (at sea level). It gets cooler at night in the mountains (especially in the higher elevations of the Blue Mountains), making it ideal for sleeping. The sun shines almost every day. Rainfall comes in the form of brief, intense cloudbursts, quickly followed by sunshine. It's pretty hard not to get a tan.

The reasons for this ideal climate are the constant temperature of the ocean—about 80 degrees F year-round—and the steady trade winds from Africa. The Caribbean is not susceptible to the harsh weather patterns of the middle latitudes. The only weather peril to a Jamaican vacation is an occasional summer tropical depression or hurricane, which can make life very exciting.

There are two basic climate categories in Jamaica: lush (very green, hot, somewhat humid, with lots of rainfall) and arid (brown with cactus and very dry). The windward side (the north and east coasts) is the lush, wetter and greener side. The mountains that traverse the island from southeast to northwest block most of the typical rainfall that comes with the prevailing trade winds. This makes the southern coast (from Kingston to Black River) semi-arid to arid. Vegetation tends scrubby with cactus, although there certainly are enough palm trees around to keep palm tree lovers happy. The western end of Jamaica is fairly lush as the mountains on this end of the island are too low to stop the rain.

Both lush and arid climes are warm to hot, depending on the season and the extent of the trade winds. Summer, while only about five degrees hotter than winter, feels much warmer due to the increased humidity and decreased wind. The one constant is the sun. It is always strong, and will swiftly fry unprotected pale faces—and bodies—to a glowing shade of lobster red.

Building a Base for Tanning

Since the advent of "fake 'n bake" (tanning machines) and pretanning accelerators, there is absolutely no reason to get burned on your first day out in the tropical sun. With some advance attention, you can stay outside for hours on your first day, and let's face it, what you want to do when you step off the plane is hit the beach.

Just about every town has a tanning center with a cutesy name like Tanfastic or Tanfasia. Most health clubs have one or two tanning "coffins" lying around, beckoning pasty skins to look healthier and more attractive in a matter of minutes. Ultraviolet tanning is fairly safe when used properly, because the UVB light doesn't have the burning rays of earlier sun lamps or, of course, the sun.

Many of these tanning centers have tanning-prep packages of 10 sessions: you start with about five minutes of "sunning" and work up to 20 or 30. Spread out over the two weeks prior to your departure, this should give you an excellent head start on a great Caribbean tan.

Pretan accelerators, available from a wide variety of manufacturers, chemically stimulate the manufacture of melanin, the pigment that darkens your skin. (Normally it takes direct exposure to the sun to start its production.) A pretan accelerator doesn't change your color or dye your skin like the QT of yesteryear (whoops, we're dating ourselves!). It prepares the skin with extra melanin so that you tan the first time out rather than burn, and much faster, too.

What to Wear and Take Along

Less is more. That's the motto to remember when packing to go to the Caribbean. Bring only what you can carry for 10 minutes at a good clip, because you'll often be schlepping your luggage for at least that time, and it's hot. If you haven't already done so, invest in a piece of luggage with wheels.

What you really need to take along are a bathing suit, shorts, T-shirts or tanks, cotton sweater, a pair of sandals, sunglasses, and a Discman. After all, you are on vacation. However, this is the dawn of a new century and people tend to dress up for no reason, so you may want to bring some extra togs to look presentable at the dinner table. To help you be totally prepared (and to make your packing a lot easier), we've assembled a list of essentials for a week.

The Packing List
Clothes
- bathing suit (or two)
- T shirts (4)—You'll end up buying at least one.
- tank tops—They're cooler and show off your muscles or curves.
- polo shirts (2)
- shorts (2)
- nice, compatible lightweight pants (also good for the plane)
- sandals—Those that can get wet, like Tevas, are best.
- cotton sweater or sweatshirt
- undergarments
- sneakers (or good walking shoes) or topsiders (for boaters)
- Women: lightweight dress (most women prefer to bring a couple of dresses for evening)
- Men: If you must have a lightweight sport coat wear it (with appropriate shoes) on the plane.

Essentials
- toiletries
- sunscreens (SPF 15+, 8, 4 [oil], and lip protector)
- moisturizers (Noxema is still the old standard for sunburn; or aloe gel)
- some good books—Don't expect to find a worthwhile read at your destination.
- Cutter's or Woodsman's insect repellent, or Skin So Soft (oh, those nasty bugs)
- sunglasses!
- hat or visor!
- Discman (CDs) or iPod
- camcorder or pocket camera (disposables are great for the beach and underwater disposables for snorkeling)
- "credit card" calculator (for exchange rates)
- Sports Accessories (where applicable)
- tennis racquet
- golf clubs

hiking shoes
fins, mask, snorkel, regulator, and C-card
ATM card and credit cards
valid passport (keep in hotel safe)
driver's license

Jamaica Superlatives

Best Beach—**Long Bay**, Portland
Best Large Luxury Resort (over 100 rooms)—**Round Hill Hotel & Villas**, Hanover
Best Small Luxury Resort (under 100 rooms)—**Strawberry Hill**, Kingston
Best Resort for Kids—**Coyaba Beach Resort**, Mo Bay
Best Romantic Hotel—**Tensing Pen**, Negril
Best Boutique Hotel— **The Caves**, Negril
Best Large Hotel—**Negril Gardens**
Best Small Hotel—**Plantation Inn**, Ochos Rios
Best Inn—**Kuyaba**, Negril
Best Eco-Friendly "Green" Hotel—**Hotel Mocking Bird Hill**, Port Antonio
Best Gay-Friendly Accommodation—**Hotel Mocking Bird Hill**, Port Antonio
Best Room with a View—**Tensing Pen**, Negril
Best Continental Restaurant—**Georgian House**, Motego Bay
Best Caribbean-Fusion Restaurant—**Norma's on the Terrace**, Kingston
Best Seafood Restaurant—**Kuyaba**, Negril
Best Jerk Pits—**Boston Bay**, Portland
Best Italian Restaurant—**Julia's**, Mo Bay
Best Asian Restaurant—**Gordon's**, Kingston
Best Steak/Burger Joint—**Jam' Rock**, Kingston
Best Vegetarian Restaurant—**Hungry Lion**, Negril
Best Lunch Spot—**Cosmo's**, Negril
Best Sunday Brunch—**Strawberry Hill**, Kingston
Best Place to Get High—**Miss Brown's**, Negril
Best Rum Punch—**Trident Hotel & Villas**, Port Antonio
Best Place for a Sunset Cocktail—**Pickled Parrot**, Negril

Best Nightclub—**Risky Business,** Negril
Best Place for Nightlife—**Negril**
Best Reggae Festival—**Reggae Sumfest,** Mo Bay
Best Diving—**Port Royal,** Kingston
Best Snorkeling—**West End,** Negril
Best Golf Course—**White Witch,** Ritz Carlton Rose Hall, Mo Bay
Best Hike—**Blue Mt. Peak**
Best Waterfall—**YS Falls**
Best Tennis—**Tryall Club,** Hanover
Best Health Club—**Swept Away Sports Complex,** Negril
Best Shopping—**Ochos Rios**
Best T-Shirt—**Bob Marley Museum,** Kingston
Best Bargain—**Kuyaba Resort,** Negril
Best-Kept Secret—**Mandeville**

The Ten Best Beaches in Jamaica

Despite its size, Jamaica has relatively few outstanding beaches. Extensive coral reefing on the south coast and development on others are the primary reasons. Here are the best:

Long Bay—Portland Parish
The most beautiful and unspoiled beach in Jamaica, this long, double crescent strand on the eastern end of Jamaica fortunately seems beyond the reach of the ubiquitous tour buses. Definitely worth the trip.

Negril Beach—Negril
Probably Jamaica's most famous beach, and deservedly so. Its seven miles of white sand is gently sloped, almost always very calm, but always very lively.

Frenchman's Cove—Port Antonio
A beautiful cove with a clear-water stream on its west side, this is a wonderful spot if you can find a time to be there when the tour buses aren't (early morning or late afternoon). Entry fee.

Bloody Bay—Negril
As with most beautiful beaches in Jamaica, development has arrived in the form of a huge all-inclusive resort. Still, it is a beautiful beach if you can find a spot away from it all. The end near Hedonism II is also a de facto nude beach.

RUM & REGGAE'S JAMAICA

San San—Port Antonio
We love this pretty beach in lush Port Antonio which caters to the area's few resorts and villas. Entry fee.

Sandy Bay—Ochos Rios
A refuge in the middle of busy Ochi, this beach caters to the guests of the Plantation Inn but is available to nonguests for a fee.

Bluefields Bay—Bluefields
This still relatively unspoiled part of Jamaica has several pretty sandy spots along its bay.

Boston Bay—Portland Parish
Down from the five-alarm jerk pits is this pretty and petite beach adorned with colorful fishing boats.

Treasure Beach—St. Elizabeth Parish
The beauty of this brown-sand beach is that the crowds here are only fishermen and their boats.

Lime Cay—Port Royal (Kingston)
Boats from Port Royal can take you to the Kingston area's finest beach (and Port Royal is pretty cool, too).

Lodging and Restaurant Key

A Note about this Guide: We have used a number of symbols and terms to indicate prices and ambiance. Here are the code breakers.

Lodging Rates

- Rates are for high season—generally mid-December through mid-April—unless otherwise noted. Summer prices are as much as 50 percent cheaper.
- The following categories correspond to rack rates for the least expensive double room. Unless otherwise noted. Rates for singles are the same or slightly less.
- Expect a service and tax charge of at least 15 percent added to your bill. Some countries can reach 25 percent! Ouch! Be sure to ask ahead of time to avoid going into shock. (Ask at the front desk how the service charge will be distributed to employees—usually you are not expected to leave any additional tips.)

☞ Be sure to ask about credit cards when making your reservations if you intend to use them as payment. A few places, even expensive ones, do not accept credit cards.

Dirt Cheap	under $50
Cheap	$51–$100
Not So Cheap	$101–$150
Pricey	$151–$200
Very Pricey	$201–$300
Wicked Pricey	$301–$400
Ridiculous	$401–$500
Beyond Belief	$501–$600
Stratospheric	$601 and up!

Meal Codes

- EP (European Plan)—No meals included.
- CP (Continental Plan)—Continental breakfast (bread, cereal, juice, coffee) included.
- BP (Breakfast Plan)—Full hot breakfast included.
- MAP (Modified American Plan)—Full breakfast and dinner included.
- FAP (Full American Plan)—Full breakfast, lunch, and dinner included (sometimes with an afternoon "tea" or snack as well).
- All-Inclusive All meals, beer, wine, and well drinks (house brands) are included, most or all on-site activities, and usually tax and service charges.

Restaurant Prices

Prices represent per-person cost for the average meal from soup to nuts.

$	$0–$10
$$	$11–$20
$$$	$21–$30
$$$$	$31–$40
$$$$$	over $40

… RUM & REGGAE'S JAMAICA …

Touristo Scale Key

(1)
What century is this?

(2)
Tiny or no airport, or political upheaval keeps tourists away.

(3)
A nice, unspoiled yet civilized place.

(4)
Still unspoiled, but getting popular.

(5)
A popular place, but still not too developed.

(6)
Busy and booming; this was very quiet not long ago.

(7)
Well-developed tourism and lots of tourists; fast-food outlets conspicuous.

(8)
Highly developed and tons of tourists.

(9)
Mega-tourists, and tour groups; fast-food outlets outnumber restaurants.

(10)
Swarms of tourists and total development. Run for cover!

RUM & REGGAE'S JAMAICA

Rum & Reggae Punch

Are you dreaming of the tropics but it's snowing outside? Don't worry, you can create your own heat with this recipe.

Ingredients
1 lime
4 oz. water
2–3 oz. good dark rum (the stronger, the better)
2 oz. sugar syrup*
bitters
ice
freshly grated nutmeg

Directions
Squeeze the lime and add the juice and water to the rum and sugar syrup in a tall glass. Shake bitters into the glass four times. Add the rocks, then sprinkle with freshly grated nutmeg (it must be fresh!). Yum! Serves one.

---

*To make sugar syrup, combine 1 lb. sugar and 2 cups of water in a saucepan. Boil for about 2 minutes for sugar to dissolve. Let cool. Keep handy for quick and easy rum punches.

JAMAICA

Touristo Scale: 🯅 🯅 🯅 🯅 🯅 🯅 🯅 🯅 🯅 (9)

Overview

IT WAS GROUP THERAPY gone postal. There we were, a motley crew of travel writers, on our first trip to Jamaica and unbeknownst to each other. We were together 24/7. By the third day, some personalities had become so abrasive that we were all on the verge of violent acts against one another. Then something happened. At first, we folks from Rum & Reggae thought that someone had spiked the rum punch with a heavy dose of Valium. But no, this was an ambient mellowing of hostile forces. Jamaica had kicked in.

Yes mon, that was a long time ago (1987). We've been back many times since and each time, without fail, Jamaica kicks in again. We've learned, however, to leave the group therapy behind (we're not great believers in group anyway). Now we travel on our own, and the natural high is that much better.

Jamaica is a big country—the island is the third largest in the Caribbean after Cuba and Hispaniola. There are many different destinations for the traveler: Montego Bay, the North Coast, Ocho Rios, Negril, Port Antonio, the South Coast, and Kingston, the island's capital. Your Jamaican experience will vary dramatically with each destination. You will be subjected to tourist hordes in Ocho Rios (called Ochi by locals), be sequestered (really locked) away in a large resort on the North Coast, and experience more tourist swarms in Montego Bay. With two exceptions, we strongly recommend avoiding Ocho Rios and the North Coast, with their tyranny of all-inclusive resorts (such as the Sandals, Couples, and the Superclub empires—Beaches, Breezes, Grand Lido and the Hedonisms). The exceptions are the Jamaica Inn, an old-time resort of character and style, and Goldeneye, another fabulous Chris Blackwell/Island Outpost venture. We would also avoid

Montego Bay (a.k.a. MoBay), except for Round Hill and Tryall—two luxury resorts just south of MoBay—and a few resorts to the east. Of course, we love Reggae Sum'Fest, held in MoBay every August. You should *definitely* go to Negril, which is fun, mellow, and what you think the Jamaican experience should be. You might also try Port Antonio, which is fairly quiet and incredibly verdant. Kingston is worth a trip for various cultural institutions, including the Bob Marley Museum (yeah, mon). The South Coast is just away from it all.

All kinds of people go to Jamaica, reflecting its size and diverse appeal. Package-tour groups go to the all-inclusive resorts, which we loathe (can you tell?) and which are bountiful in Jamaica. These are resorts where everything—room, meals, drinks, tips, and all kinds of activities—is included in one price. All-inclusives are, with a few exceptions, just a muddle of mediocrity, down to the last buffet dinner. Their clientele is generally not terribly sophisticated, but they are easily satisfied and very budget-conscious. Their attitude is, "Why should I go out for a lunch, dinner, or drinks when it's free here? "(It really isn't—they've already paid for it.) But this thinking locks them in, and all-inclusive tourists rarely leave the front gates unless it's on a tour bus. We find this very sad. It also creates bad vibes with the locals, especially the merchants. The "let 'em out for two hours to shop" bus trip leaves local vendors and merchants little time to market their wares and increases the pressure on them to sell, as this is the way they make a living. The result is that they tend to aggressively hawk their goods, much to the terror of fear-fed tourists, who have heard all the negative stories about Jamaica. Thus a cycle of fear, resentment, and misunderstanding is perpetuated and exacerbated by these walled prisons called all-inclusives.

Even worse than the all-inclusive resorts are the couples-only all-inclusive resorts, like Couples (which, until recently, used two fornicating lions as their logo—subtle, huh?). The very thought of staying at one of these places gives us hives! Can you imagine being stuck with hundreds of other couples gathered around the buffet table? We'd rather die. And then there is Hedonism II & III, which are trips in themselves In sum, the all-inclusives are really just adult summer camps with double rooms instead of bunkhouses, and aerobics and crab races replacing arts and crafts. They are great for people for whom luxury is a fiberglass hot tub, an open bar with house brands, or "ethnic night" in the dining room.

The younger, more with-it crowd heads for Negril. This is where Jamaicans go to unwind, and unwound it is. Situated on the west coast of the island with a seven-mile-long golden beach, Negril is a beehive of laid-back vibes. A good mood prevails here, probably because everyone is so high. The very relaxed atmosphere is reflected by the mildly laissez-faire attitude of the local government toward *ganja* (marijuana) and "magic" mushrooms (the ones that make you laugh hysterically and sometimes give you mild hallucinations). While still illegal and punishable with stiff fines and prison sentences, both are easily available in Negril. At many local (i.e., Jamaican) restaurants, you can order a spliff for dessert (it's not on the menu, however) or a steaming cup of mushroom tea.

Those seeking a quiet and wonderfully lush setting can explore Port Antonio. This was Jamaica's first resort area, made famous by Errol Flynn—who had a residence here—and turned the banana boats into the island's first tourist attraction. There are some magnificent cove beaches here, hidden by really tropical vegetation. Many films requiring an idyllic tropical location were shot here, including *Cocktail, Club Paradise, Lord of the Flies, Return to Treasure Island, Clara's Heart,* and *The Mighty Quinn*. Ironically, Port Antonio is now one of the least-touristy Jamaica destinations, which is why we like it. However, this area has rested too long on its glamorous-past laurels. Most of the lodgings here are in need of a face-lift or a shot of dollars, and their relatively high rates don't equate with the product delivered.

Finally, for reggae and art lovers, there is Kingston. Here you'll find the Bob Marley Museum—a must stop—and numerous art galleries where you can buy Jamaican art. There is also the Institute of Jamaica and the National Gallery, the latter the best showcase for a lesson in Jamaican art, past and present. As the largest English-speaking city south of Miami, Kingston is big (population 800,000), so a day is all you'll need here, unless you like big cities.

Note: Many prospective visitors to Jamaica are alarmed by the island's reputation for violent crime—Kingston, in particular, is known for its appalling murder rate. However, it's important to stress that visitors touring Jamaica are unlikely to encounter any serious misfortune, particularly if they take the precautions one would exercise at home in an urban area. West Kingston is a dangerous neighborhood, and some parts of Montego Bay are not safe after dusk. Political unrest does occur from time to time, although the bulk of the conflict is usually acted out in the capital (if you plan to spend time in Kingston, check with the U.S. State Department for the latest advisories: http://travel.state.gov/travel_warnings.html). Otherwise, use common sense, keep your car doors locked when traveling at night through urban areas, and seek out the recommendations made by the hotels listed in this guide.

The Briefest History of a Complex Country

Jamaica was settled by the Arawaks, who had a peaceful agrarian society. The name Jamaica comes from the Arawak *Xaymaca*, which means "Land of Wood and Water." The fierce Caribs never made it here, but the Spanish did, beginning with Columbus's sighting of Jamaica on his second voyage, in 1494. They established a capital in 1509 near Ocho Rios and named it New Seville, which today is being excavated by archeologists. They began sugarcane cultivation and introduced slavery, first with the Arawaks. It didn't take long for the Arawaks to be wiped out (there were about 100,000 when the Spaniards arrived), so the Spanish then imported Africans. Many of the slaves escaped into the mountains and later became known as the Maroons, from the Spanish word *cimarrones*, "runaways."

In 1655 the English drove out the Spaniards and proceeded to take the production of sugar and the importation of slaves to new heights. The English also encouraged pirates (Henry Morgan was one) to operate out of Port Royal, on the peninsula outside Kingston. They plundered Spanish and French ships and established Port Royal as "the richest, wickedest city in Christendom." The honeymoon ended in 1692, when a catastrophic earthquake caused much of the city literally to fall into the sea. Divine intervention, perhaps? Today there are still some buildings left and Port Royal is an interesting stop if you are in the Kingston area.

Meanwhile, the Maroons were giving the British major headaches, periodically staging rebellions and attracting more runaway slaves. Frustrated, the British granted the Maroons autonomy in 1739, which they still have today, although the Maroons are also full-fledged Jamaican citizens. The planters, following the lead of the American revolutionaries, were getting restless. However, the towering presence of Lord Nelson and the British Navy in the West Indies squelched the discontent.

In 1834 slavery was abolished in the British Empire. Economic turmoil followed, but with the importation of Indians (from India) and Chinese as indentured servants, sugar and rum production continued in Jamaica, albeit with reduced success. Intermarriage created the mixed racial makeup you find on the island today; hence the national motto "Out of Many, One People." Other products were developed and exported, including bananas, ginger, allspice, coffee, and bauxite.

In the 20th century, the current political scene emerged with the creation of rival parties in the 1930s: the Jamaica Labor Party (JLP), founded by Alexander Bustamante, and the People's National Party (PNP), by Norman Manley. (They were cousins, by the way.) Jamaica was one of the first British West Indies to gain independence, which was granted in 1962 with these two parties in control of the government. Rivalries between the parties became very bitter and continue to this day, although elections aren't as violent as they used to be. At issue is patronage and jobs, and each party seems to control a large army of thugs who stir things up and occasionally get violent when intimidating the other side and the voting populace at large. The worst of this occurred in the late 1970s and in early 1980 when hundreds were killed prior to the elections held on October 30, 1980. This precipitated the historic Bob Marley "One Love" concert, held in Kingston in 1978, where he got the two rival leaders to hold hands on stage. Bob's song "One Love/People Get Ready" was written for that occasion. Today the PNP is in power, but Bob's legacy for harmony seems to have caught on. Yah, mon!

Jamaica: Key Facts

LOCATION	18°N by 77°W
	90 miles south of Cuba
	1,450 miles south of New York
SIZE	4,411 square miles
	146 miles long by 22 to 51 miles wide
HIGHEST POINT	Blue Mountain Peak (7,402 ft.)
POPULATION	2.5 million
LANGUAGE	English
TIME	Eastern Standard Time all year
AREA CODE	876
ELECTRICITY	110 volts AC, 50 cycles; 220 volts in some places; ask for a transformer and adapter if necessary
CURRENCY	Jamaican dollar (J$46 = U.S.$1)
DRIVING	On the *left*; a valid driver's license from back home is acceptable for short-term visits
DOCUMENTS	U.S. and Canadian citizens need proof of citizenship with a photo ID, plus an ongoing or return ticket; other visitors need passports
DEPARTURE TAX	$27
BEER TO DRINK	Red Stripe
RUM TO DRINK	Wray & Nephew Overproof
MUSIC TO HEAR	Reggae/Dancehall—Yah mon!
TOURISM INFO	800-JAMAICA or 212-856-9727
	www.jamaicatravel.com

Getting There

There are two international gateways: Montego Bay's Sangster International Airport and Kingston's Norman Manley International Airport. The MoBay airport gets the bulk of the tourist arrivals (MoBay is equidistant between Negril and Ocho Rios; driving times are noted under "Getting Around," below).

Air Jamaica flies to Montego Bay and Kingston from Washington D.C., Ft. Lauderdale, Miami, Orlando, New York–JFK, Atlanta,

Philadelphia, Newark, Boston, and Baltimore; and to MoBay only from Los Angeles, Chicago, and Houston. **American Airlines** serves MoBay and Kingston from Miami and New York–JFK; **Northwest Airlines** flies in to MoBay from Memphis and Detroit (winter only); and **USAirways** serves MoBay from Charlotte and Philadelphia.

Air Jamaica and **British Airways** fly to Jamaica from London, and **Air Canada** flies between Toronto and MoBay and Kingston. **ALM** flies to the island from Curacao, **BWIA** serves Jamaica from Antigua, Barbados and Trinidad, and **Cayman Airways** flies in from Grand Cayman. There are small airports at Negril, Ocho Rios and Port Antonio served by **Air Jamaica Express** puddle-jumpers from MoBay and Kingston; **Air Negril** also makes the link between MoBay and Negril.

Getting Around

Since Jamaica is a big country, you'll want to rent a car if you plan to venture far. If you're based in Negril, you probably won't need a car if you plan to just stay there. There are plenty of cabs to take you around in Negril (average cab fare is $5). But if you really want to explore, rent a car. The roads are in surprisingly good shape by Caribbean standards, but watch out for the local drivers—they go very fast. Most of the major car-rental agencies have outposts here, including **Budget** (800-527-0700) and **Hertz** (800-654-3131). As rentals here are among the most expensive in the Caribbean, be sure to call around and reserve well ahead of your trip to get the best rate. Also note that most American auto insurance policies *specifically* exclude coverage for driving in Jamaica—be sure to obtain insurance with your rental.

If you prefer not to rent a car and you're traveling beyond the two major airports, note that the one-way taxi fare from MoBay to Negril is upwards of $100. Licensed taxis all have red "PPV" plates —if the vehicle you are getting into does not have these plates, it is not likely to be insured (they're known locally as "robots"), and you'll probably end up sharing it with others going your way. Once you spend a few days here, you'll see how some drivers seem to have a death wish, so be very cautious about using unlicensed taxis. Always agree on a price before entering the taxi.

Alternatively, **Jamaica Tours** (876-953-3700) has regular bus service between major points—the trip from the MoBay airport to Negril is $20. Or you can use the frequent and highly informal minibus service that connects the island's major and minor destinations; MoBay-Negril is about $3. These minibuses will often be crammed with up to 20 people, which can create a real squeeze with your luggage, but they are a true Jamaican experience, speeding between major towns, and with the bass boom of impressive sound systems pounding away. When you spot your destination, call out "One stop, driver!" and he'll pull over and collect your fare. Since most people travel via road to their resort destination(s), here are driving times between the major points:

> Negril: 90 minutes from MoBay
>
> Ocho Rios: 2 hours from either MoBay or Kingston
>
> Port Antonio: 2 hours from Kingston, 4 hours from MoBay
>
> Treasure Beach: 90 minutes from MoBay, 3 hours from Kingston

There used to be a train from Montego Bay to Kingston, which took five hours and was an amazing trip. We highly recommended it in the first edition of *Rum & Reggae Caribbean*. However, it runs no more—a real shame.

Focus on Jamaica: Sex and Drugs and Reggae, Mon!

In our opinion (and we are *very* opinionated), there are only certain destinations in Jamaica worth visiting for the aforementioned reasons: Negril; Round Hill, Tryall, and Half Moon near Montego Bay; the Jamaica Inn in Ocho Rios; Port Antonio; the South Coast; and Kingston. These options offer plenty and are the best of scores. One caveat: Jamaica is inundated with spring breakers during February–March, particularly MoBay and Negril. If a 24-hour frat-house scene and relentless thump of music into the wee hours isn't your style, don't visit these towns during this period.

Negril—All Your Brain and Body Needs

There is a resort in Negril called Hedonism II—one of the pervasive all-inclusives that are overwhelming Jamaica—which has established itself as the premier party place in the Caribbean. The tales emanating from here are mind-boggling, if they are indeed for real. Stories abound of people going at it in public. And not only in the usual places like hot tubs, but in the middle of the dining pavilion . . . while dinner is being served. Maybe it's the name that makes everyone feel naughty. Whatever, this is adult summer camp at its raunchiest.

There is also a place in Negril called Miss Brown's, where you can get "magic" mushroom tea and "special" cake (not unlike the brownies we used to make in college), as well as more down-to-earth fare. There are two strengths of tea, regular and double. May we suggest the regular-strength tea (about $3), as it will give you quite a buzz. For those of you who still don't get it (a reader told us she didn't know what "special" cake was, tried it, and was surprised and unhappy that she got high—c'mon, coffee, smell it!), "special" cake is cake made with marijuana and "magic" mushrooms that will make you laugh hysterically and sometimes will be mildly hallucinogenic. Now you know. Anyway, Miss Brown's is really a must stop. A visit here will definitely put a smile on your face. Located about a half-mile east of the roundabout that separates the Beach from the West End, it's a typical small, spartan Jamaican restaurant with more on the menu than jerk chicken. It is run by warm and modest country folk who are perfectly comfortable with inquisitive travelers who seek out their "cafe." So it's somewhat surprising when Miss Brown hands out attractive business cards describing her place as "World Famous," although maybe by now it is. The logo on the card is, of course, mushrooms. She even sells T-shirts with the same logo.

Sex and drugs—all that's missing is rock 'n roll. As Ian Dury (of the Blockheads) once sang, "It's all me brain and body needs." If you replace rock 'n roll with reggae, you should be very happy in Negril, the land of anything goes. Now don't get me wrong—Negril is not one huge bacchanalia (unless you stay at Hedonism II). It's just an extremely mellow place where rules and regulations seem to evaporate in the tropical heat. The quintessence of laid-back, the ambiance here is not some developer's contrivance but its own natural karma. We've never experienced anything quite like it. This is where Jamaicans go to relax, and they're already a helluva lot more relaxed than we are. So if you need to cool out at your own pace (without feeling programmed), this is the place to do it. Or if you're a believer in sunbathing in the buff, it's no problem here.

There are actually two parts to Negril, the Beach and the West End. The Beach is a seven-mile arc of sand, calm turquoise water, and palm trees. It is highly developed, but in Negril fashion. While the last few years have seen the development of several huge all-inclusive resorts, including the Grand Lido, Sandals, Beaches, and a Couples brands, one of the few rules in Negril that *is* followed is a strict building code that dictates that no building can rise higher than the trees (although we think a few crafty developers brought in very tall trees from elsewhere in order to build an extra story). The Beach itself is very public, making Negril one of the few destinations in Jamaica where tourists and Jamaicans can mingle freely without security gates, guards, and the heightened racial consciousness that accompanies such barriers. The Beach is also a moving bazaar, with all kinds of goods and services brought to your beach towel or chaise for scrutiny. You will never really want for anything. Fresh fruit, sodas, beer, nuts, *ganja*—all the refreshments that make for a great beach day—are available cheaply with a simple wave of the hand. If you are already taken care of, then a pleasant "no, thank you" will keep the traffic moving. Despite all of this human commotion, the Beach's beauty is mostly intact. And the sand extends way out, creating a natural swimming pool of very clear water. The shoreline is shallow, which allows you to go far out before you're over your head.

The West End is a rocky peninsula that juts out from the southern end of the Beach. It is the funkier, hippie-ish section of town. Here you'll find lots of Rasta vegetarian restaurants, bars and rum shops, as well as local arts, crafts, some excellent accommodations, and some very popular hangouts, including the Pickled Parrot. When the sun sets, the Beach is home to the reggae party places: Alfred's, Roots Bamboo, DeBuss, and Risky Business. Rick's Cafe, located well down the West End Road, is very popular for sunset cocktails and is probably the biggest *tourist* attraction in Negril. It is also where local boys dive off the cliffs to the clicks of scores of cameras.

Kingston—Rastaman Vibrations, Yeah (Positive)

*You're going to lively up yourself and
    don't be no drag,
You're going to lively up yourself 'cause reggae is
    another bag.
You lively up yourself and don't say no,
You're gonna lively up yourself 'cause I said so.*

Thus spake Bob Marley. As the undisputed king of reggae, his 1974 song "Lively Up Yourself" was a call to action on behalf of Jamaica's biggest export—his music. At the peak of his career, his record sales accounted for about 10 percent of the country's gross national product. Even after his premature death in 1981, he is still considered the prime mover in popularizing reggae in North America and throughout the world.

Bob Marley is a national hero. His statue stands in the middle of a square across from the National Arena in Kingston, a tribute to his contribution not only to Jamaican music but to his country's cultural identity. But as reggae music goes, he is certainly not the only Jamaican to leave his or her mark. There is Bob's son, Ziggy, with the Melody Makers and Judy Mowatt—a former member of the Wailers female vocal backup, the I-Threes. Bunny Wailer and the late Peter Tosh, both former members of the Wailers, were known worldwide. So are Jimmy Cliff, Gregory Isaacs, Freddie "Toots" (of the Maytalls), Sister Carol, Burning Spear, Nadine Sutherland, Terror Fabulous, Shabba Ranks, Beenie Man, Buju Banton, General B, and the bands Third World, Black Uhuru, and Chalice. There are countless more. A visit to a Kingston record shop will reveal more artists you've never even heard of, and a huge selection of 45s (from local talent and labels), which we haven't seen since the '60s. Surprisingly, two well-known reggae bands are not Jamaican—UB40 and Steel Pulse are British, although some of these groups' band members trace their roots to Jamaica.

Reggae now has a strong following around the world, and recent reggae bands like Ziggy Marley and the Melody Makers, Shabba

Ranks, and UB40 have been hugely successful. Bob Marley's *Legend* album, a collection of his work first released in 1984, is still selling like crazy. Final proof of reggae's popularity is its offspring, dancehall—a reggae-rap hybrid—which has swept through the Caribbean, the U.S., and Europe on the popularity of artists like Beenie Man.

It didn't used to be that way, even when Bob Marley was king (many say he still is). Reggae's success was a long time coming. The music first hit the charts in 1969, when Desmond Dekker reached number 12 on the Billboard chart with "The Israelites." Jimmy Cliff then had a hit in 1970 with "Wonderful World, Beautiful People." Bob Marley and the Wailers' 1976 album, *Rastaman Vibration*, reached number 8 on the Billboard album charts—which at the time was unprecedented for both Marley and reggae musicians in general.

On the other hand, "mainstream" musicians have made it big with reggae. Paul Simon led the way when he wrote "Mother and Child Reunion" back in 1972. About the same time, Johnny Nash took Bob Marley's song "Stir It Up," made it a hit, and followed shortly thereafter with the reggae-influenced "I Can See Clearly Now." Then came Eric Clapton's blockbuster version of "I Shot the Sheriff"—another Marley tune. After that, a number of groups jumped on the reggae bandwagon, from The Police with songs like "Roxanne" to such all-time greats as Bonnie Raitt ("One Belief Away"). Newer artists, like Lauren Hill and Sugar Ray, have recently had hits using the reggae or dancehall format.

Reggae's Roots

Reggae evolved from a variety of Jamaican musical styles. Its roots can be heard in the traditional Jamaican music called "mento." It has a slow beat and rather lewd lyrics—much like the beguine of Martinique. Like the "wine" and calypso music, it was danced very intimately, with two people joined at the hips simulating intercourse.

The advent of rhythm and blues in the U.S., coupled with the spread of transistor radios, doomed mento. The powerful AM broadcasts out of Miami brought the R&B sound home to Jamaica. So did the growing popularity of "sound systems"—traveling DJs with PA systems and the hottest singles from the U.S. American music soon influenced Jamaica's own, resulting in a fast-paced synthesis called "ska."

While ska was not tremendously popular elsewhere, Millie Small's 1964 song "My Boy Lollipop" was a worldwide hit. By the late '60s, ska gave way to yet another music called "rock steady." It was much slower, with a more evenly paced beat—reggae's forerunner. Rock steady delivered an increasingly more serious message than its lighthearted predecessor. The music soon expressed the heightened sense of black pride brought on by the U.S. civil rights and Black Power movements.

It was rock steady's growing lyrical consciousness that gave birth to the slower, more powerful reggae. Reggae became the vehicle of discontent, rooted in the shantytowns of West Kingston and Trenchtown. Bob Marley and the Wailers became the stewards of this new music, formulating the now-familiar guitar rhythms and timing. In 1970 Marley founded the Tuff Gong Studios, and by 1971 he and his band were on their way with the hit "Trenchtown Rock." At the time of his death in 1981 at age 36(of brain cancer), Marley had produced more than 20 albums and had made reggae a dynamic force worldwide.

While reggae is still popular on the Jamaican scene, dancehall now reigns supreme. Beenie Man, Mr. Vegas, and Bounty Killa are three of the most popular dancehall artists at the moment.

The Bob Marley Museum, 56 Hope Road, Kingston 6, Jamaica, W.I. Local: 876-927-9152.

This is a must stop in Jamaica for any reggae fan. Run by Rastas, it occupies the former Tuff Gong Studios, where most of Bob Marley and the Wailers' best music was recorded. It's located in a well-heeled neighborhood near Jamaica House (the official residence of the prime minister). When you pull up to the gate, you are greeted by a security guard who announces that the only pictures allowed are of the Marley statue inside. After that, all cameras and recording devices must be checked at the gatehouse. A guide will then take you inside to view an hourlong video presentation that shows Bob Marley in concert, recording at the studio (which is where you are sitting), and out and about. The rest of the tour includes the grounds, notably murals, herb gardens, Marley's statue, a beehive, and a real live *ganja* plant.

Back inside the museum, which originally was an old Victorian house, there are two floors of memorabilia. They include two rooms of news clippings pasted to the walls, a replica of Bob's first record shop in Trenchtown, called Wail 'n Soul Records, his bedroom preserved intact (it looks like a hippie den—with pillows on the floor and a large smoking pipe), as well as a wax statue à la Madame Tussaud that one of these days will move to simulate him singing. When you finish the tour, you'll want to check out the souvenir shop for T-shirts and jewelry.

Admission is $8 for adults, and hours are 9:30 A.M. to 4 P.M. daily. Closed Sunday.

Reggae SumFest

Now here is an event for hard-core reggae and dancehall fans. Held each summer (there have been more than 18, including the old Reggae Sunsplash), this five-day festival always features the best talent in the field—a mini-Woodstock of reggae music. Held in Montego Bay, the Sunsplash venue was moved briefly to Kingston in 1993, which proved very unpopular (no beaches and not enough tourist facilities) and led to the demise of Reggae Sunsplash. Now called Reggae SumFest (new producers), the festival returned to Montego Bay and is held at Catherine Hall. This event regularly draws over 120,000 people during the course of the festival.

Daily admission to the events is $12-$35, but weekly passes are also available, which include special entry and unlimited access to all SumFest events, a souvie 'zine, and access to the backstage hospitality area and parking. Many packages include these passes and lodging, airfare, etc. For more info, call 800-JAMAICA or visit the official Web site at: www.reggaesumfest.com, where you'll find tour operator packages, many including airfare from the U.S.

Other Cool Jamaican Stuff

Jamaican Art

There are few places in the Caribbean where the art scene is as dynamic or impressive as it is in Jamaica. This can readily be seen in Kingston, the island's capital. The average tourist may think that the crafts markets of Ocho Rios or Montego Bay, with their wood carvings and amateur paintings, encapsulate the Jamaican art scene. But this is hardly the case.

For a true perspective on Jamaican art, you must visit the **National Gallery,** Roy West Building, Kingston Mall (876-922-8540). Since 1982 the gallery has occupied two floors of this building—and it has already outgrown them. Its 18 galleries house various collections of paintings, prints, and sculptures from different eras and artists of Jamaica. The gallery also has an international collection that focuses on Caribbean works.

Of particular interest at the gallery is the magnificent sculpture collection of Edna Manley, one of the primary forces in modern Jamaican art. Her work is truly moving, from the reflection on political violence called *Ghetto Mother* (1982) to such timeless pieces as *Negro Aroused* (1935), *The Beadseller* (1922), *The Diggers* (1936), and *Horse of the Morning* (1943).

There are other prominent artists whose works should not be missed. These include Mallica Reynolds (known as Kapo), Barrington Watson, Christopher Gonzalez, Karl Parboosingh, and Albert Huie. Kapo is probably Jamaica's most prolific primitive sculptor, with evocative pieces like *All Women Are Five Women* (1965). He is also a renowned painter. Barrington Watson's neorealist oil paintings of the human form are outstanding, including *Conversation* (1981) and *Mother and Child* (1968). Christopher Gonzalez's mahogany sculpture titled *Man Arisen* (1966) explodes with emotion. *Ras Smoke I* (1972), by Karl Parboosingh, and *The Constant Spring Road* (1964), by Albert Huie, both oils, are powerful documentation of the lives and times of the Jamaican people. The Gallery is open Tuesday through Friday, 10 A.M. to 4:30 P.M., Saturday from 10 A.M. to 3 P.M., closed Sunday and Monday. Admission is $1. What a deal!

If you are in the mood to buy or browse, check out the **Contemporary Arts Centre** at 1 Liguanea Avenue (927-9958); **The Edna Manley School of the Visual Arts** at the Cultural Training Centre, 1 Arthur Wint Drive, with works in progress and a student exhibition during the last week in June and the first week of July (926-2800); the **Bolivar Bookshop and Gallery,** 1-D Grove Road (926-

8799); **Chelsea Art Gallery,** 12 Chelsea Avenue (929-2231 or 929-0045); **Mutual Life Gallery,** 2 Oxford Road (929-4302); **Frame Centre Gallery,** 10 Tangerine Place (926-4644); **Art Gallery Ltd.,** the Hilton Hotel, 77 Knutsford Boulevard (960-8939); and finally the **Institute of Jamaica,** 12 East Street, with exhibitions by students of all ages (922-0620).

No art adventure in Kingston would be complete without seeing the monumental wall murals on the campus of the **University of the West Indies.** While there, pick up a catalog. Who knows, the Jamaican art experience may arouse new interests that demand further study.

Montego Bay—Greens by the Sea

Montego Bay—aka MoBay—is Jamaica's second largest and least interesting town. However, it is the island's de facto tourism hub (the airport here is the region's second-busiest, after San Juan), with lots of hotels, and Negril and Ocho Rios less than two hours away by road. But there is one reason to stay in MoBay: for the excellent golf. There are five 18-hole courses in the area surrounding the city—two of them outstanding—making MoBay one of the Caribbean's top golf destinations. Here's an overview, starting with our favorite.

Located about 20 minutes east of MoBay, near Round Hill, **Tryall** is one of the finest and prettiest courses in the Caribbean. Indeed, one guest we talked to was on his 15th visit and preferred the Tryall course to Pebble Beach. A superbly maintained and scenic par-71, it has in the past accommodated the Johnny Walker World Championship and the Mazda Championship. The course is a hilly 6,920 yards (Championship) and is full of water hazards on the last holes, especially the tricky 15th, a par-3. There are two par-5s that each are 500 yards or over. The course is tough and challenging, with wind from the sea and thick roughs, but it's also beautiful—signs of the property's glory days are everywhere, including the plantation's 200-year-old waterwheel. Views of the turquoise sea are a backdrop to every divot.

Named after Annee Palmer, the notorious mistress of Rose Hall Plantation in the 19th century, the **White Witch** course is Jamaica's newest, and some say it's the best in the islands. The fairway is designed by Robert van Hagge and it climbs up and down the abrupt hillsides overlooking the affiliated Ritz-Carlton resort—a fortune is spent keeping it up-to-snuff. The White Witch is 6,800 yards (Championship), and native stone inlaid walls shore up the greens and tees on many holes. However, it's a tough course, with dramatic elevation changes, and it can make the average player feel like a maladroit goon. But you can also count on breathtaking sea views and fresh, cool wind at this elevation. Plus, being a Ritz-Carlton, the resort assigns a "golf concierge" (oh puh-*leeze!*) to every group, who will retrieve wayward shots, advise on club selection, and keep balls burnished and bright. That's called a caddie where we play golf.

The **Wyndham Rose Hall** course is designed by Ian Smedley, and full of twists, hills, dips and water hazards. It benefits from a recent, and significant, infusion of money. Starting at an attractive English colonial-style clubhouse containing the requisite dining room and bar (and with the added flourish of a cannon in the courtyard), this uncompromising course of 6,598 yards (Championship) starts you off with a par-5 hook left that could wreck the rest of your game. The third hole, while short, requires you to place the ball over a pond about as big as the fairway; it ends only feet from the green. The eighth hole is considered the hardest; the left side is on the crashing surf and the green is a blind hole left of the tee. The back nine is full of obstacles and requires real skill to finesse the ball to several blind greens. The 14th and 15th holes are twin toughies—the former features an uphill battle and a very tight right angle to the green; the latter has water hazards, including a waterfall, both fore and aft of the green (it was used in the 007 film *Live and Let Die*). Wyndham Rose Hall has a great driving range, which slopes downhill and is set against the surf rolling in the distance.

Designed by Robert Trent Jones in 1961, the **Half Moon** course is another well maintained par-72, but easier and less dynamic than the previous three. With a more traditional links layout, it is long and narrow at 7,143 yards (Championship) and consists mainly of straight fairways—it's a power hitter's dream. There are four par-5 holes that will keep your drivers very busy, while the greens are defended by all-embracing bunkers. A fifth course, **Ironshore**, is shorter, cheaper and enveloped by villas and condos.

Where to Stay
Negril

In Negril there are more options for lodging, from rustic and funky to deluxe megaresort, than in practically any other part of Jamaica. You can choose according to your style and budget, but the offbeat type of accommodation is still a Negril specialty. If you stay on the West End—the location of the first four hotels—there is no beach, but you get to dive into turquoise water from rock platforms—lots of fun and no sand to stick to your legs.

The West End

Tensing Pen, P.O. Box 3013, West End Road, Negril, Jamaica, W.I. Local: 876-957-0387, fax 876-957-0161.
Web site: www.tensingpen

Situated on a rocky bluff on the West End amid several acres of lushly landscaped grounds, Tensing Pen is our favorite place to stay in Negril. The accommodations are truly fabulous for their uniqueness, privacy, and setting. Looking like primitive thatched huts, the wood, thatch, and cut stone cottages are actually quite elegantly, if simply, furnished with four-poster mosquito-netted beds, polished wood floors, and private bath. There is a lanai with rocking chairs, most looking out over the water, facing west. We couldn't think of a better place in Negril to sit and read or watch for the green flash. Many of the huts are elevated, called the Pillars, giving the impression of a tree house. These also have outdoor showers—a fabulous touch in the tropics. Two favorites are Middle Pillar and Cove Cottage. All the units have privileges in a well-equipped communal kitchen attached to a very comfortable and pleasant dining and sitting area. For large groups, there is a three-bedroom Great House with a huge living room: it is basically open to the sea and the views. The staff is very friendly and willing to help with any special needs.

While Tensing Pen doesn't have a beach, it has a craggy coastline with all kinds of places to jump or dive into the crystal-clear turquoise water and strategically placed ladders to get out easily. On most days the water is very calm, making it fun and safe to do so. There are also sunning patios carved out of the rock, with chaises for your tanning pleasure. A cove bisects the property and a footbridge connects the two points, although it is not necessary to use the bridge. It doesn't have any railings and is sort of like walking a wide plank over the water—easy but a tad scary. Small children would not agree with Tensing Pen. Breakfast is served daily in an attractive communal kitchen. At night, guests may use the kitchen, although several times a week, the chef will prepare a full dinner.

Rates are *Not So Cheap* (CP).

Catcha Falling Star, P.O. Box 13, West End Road, Negril, Jamaica, W.I. Local: 876-957-0390.

Located next door, Catcha Falling Star is a place to try if you can't get into Tensing Pen. While it lacks Tensing Pen's charm and specialness, Catcha Falling Star is still comfortable and pleasant. There are six attractive one- and two-bedroom cottages with maid service and breakfast served on your veranda. As with its neighbor, you can swim off the rocks and sun on the specially built patios. Clothes-optional bathing is an added plus.

Rates are *Pricey* and up (BP).

The Caves, P.O. Box 15, Lighthouse Road, West End, Negril, Jamaica, W.I. Stateside: 800-688-7678. Local: 876-957-0270, fax 876-957-4930.
Web site: www.islandoutpost.com
e-mail: thecaves@islandoutpost.com

It was bound to happen. With the opening of Island Outpost's Caves resort, attitude arrived in Negril. Located on the West End just south of the Negril Lighthouse, this small property of 10 cottages caters to celebutants and their entourages. Owner Chris Blackwell (of Island Records) knows what these people want in a vacation hideaway, namely luxury, hipness, design, and privacy. Keeping these in mind, he always gets his musician, model, and actor friends to patronize his establishments. They create a chichi buzz and welcome publicity, lending his places an air of exclusivity and fabulousness (the same thing happens in St. Barts). They also bring their "I'm, like, way cool" attitude, which permeates right down to the staff (we were scrutinized by the management to a degree that almost felt like a stripsearch!). Shortly after The Caves opened, Jimmy Buffet paid a visit in his seaplane. As he was landing, the local police opened fire on the plane from the nearby Negril Lighthouse, thinking it was a drug shipment from somewhere. Mr. B. wrote a song about the bullet-dodging incident called "*Jamaica Mistaka.*" Talk about an entrance!

For all this carping, you'd think The Caves would be our last resort in Negril. Not at all. Island Outpost's boutique hotels (there are others in Jamaica, the Bahamas, and Miami's South Beach) are a welcome counterpoint to the depersonalized mega all-inclusive resorts that are swallowing up Jamaica and threatening the entire Caribbean. While technically an all-inclusive (meals, fruit juice and alcohol bar, tax and service charges are included in the room rates), the atmosphere at The Caves is hardly that. Activities are kept to a minimum, except for the Aveda spa, with probably the most soothing massage room in Jamaica. There are no pool aerobics here, only a gorgeous saltwater pool built at cliff's edge (a hot tub seems to dangle over the water). The mood is serene and discreet, with a staff chosen for its looks and sophistication. Ambient music from the Island Records catalog wafts through the grounds. A stairway of coral stone descends into the huge cavern directly below the pool, where benches have been carved in the rock and night lighting adds a sense of drama to a midnight caress. The cottages are groovy in décor (handmade furniture, batik fabrics, and bright colors), although some, like Moonshadow, seem to be a tad tight in the space department (we got the feeling of being on a boat, down to the berthlike sofas and dinette). Another, called Blue Hole, has polished concrete floors and an indoor shower and bed combination as focal point (very apropos for hot and heavy couples).

Rates are **Beyond Belief!** (FAP, plus drinks, tax, and service). The entire property can be rented for a week for $7,000 a night.

Rockhouse, P.O. Box 3024. West End Road, Negril, Jamaica, W.I. Local: 876-957-4373, fax 876-957-0557.
Web site: www.rockhousehotel.com
e-mail: info@rockhousehotel.com

This is Negril's original cliff-side dwelling. The 28-room inn started in 1969, but it needed major refurbishing when a trio of Aussies took over in 1994. Today, the original thatch-roof bungalows remains, some with private outdoor showers, and you can still dive straight into the water from wooden bridges spanning the cliffs (the water here is clear and calm). But Rockhouse now also claims the chic milieu of a rugged boutique resort, without the wallet wallop. A strikingly incongruous modern pool has been built at one end of the property, and the restaurant has been upgraded; room service is now available, and all the rooms have minibars. Least expensive rooms are a septet in a two-story building back from the cliff—not much of a view, but these are a good buy.

Doubles are **Not So Cheap** (EP).

Seven Mile Beach

White Sands, P.O. Box 60., Norman Manley Boulevard, Negril, Jamaica, W.I. Local: 876-957-4291, fax 876-957-4674
Web site: www.whitesandsjamaica.com
e-mail: whitesands@cwjamaica.com

A great beachfront value, White Sands is a casual but well-run, 40-unit property that sprawls over two sides of the road. Least expensive rooms are not on the beach side—they have simple appeal and the upper units are preferable for their cathedral ceilings and balconies. Deluxe units on the beach side are just a few steps from the sand. There's a garden pool, screeching parrots and a beach bar and grill. One family has owned this spot since 1971, and though informal and glitz-free, it does have one claim to fame: Cher and Gregg Allman stayed here on their honeymoon.

Doubles are **Cheap** (EP).

Negril Cabins Resort, P.O. Box 118, Norman Manley Boulevard, Negril, Jamaica, W.I. Stateside: 800-382-3444. Local: 876-957-5350, fax 876-957-5381.
Web site: www.negril-cabins.com

On the north end of Negril across the road from the Bloody Bay beach (a truly gorgeous strand and Negril's nude beach just to the right), these tree house–like accommodations sit in a shady grove of Jamaican royal palms and bull thatch. A dramatic entrance and loggia with several fountains, beautiful wood, lush vegetation, coral stone floors, and comfortable seating areas create a cool and soothing welcome for guests. There are 86 units in 43 timber cottages. All units are comfortably furnished, very airy and open with lots of blond wood, wide-board floors, and colorful upholstery. Each unit has a private balcony or patio, ceiling fan, and private bath (Superior rooms have air conditioning and cable TV). Windows are louvered with screens. The beach across the road is owned by the resort and has lots of shade trees. Unfortunately, a pair of all-inclusive resorts have opened next to it (there goes the neighborhood!). When making reservations, ask for a unit as far away from the road as possible; these will be the quietest. Negril Cabins is very popular with Germans and Italians.

Rates are *Not So Cheap* (EP).

Kuyaba Resort, P.O. Box 2635, Norman Manley Boulevard, Negril, Jamaica, W.I. Local: 876-957-4318, fax 876-957-9765.
Web site: www.kuyaba.com
e-mail: kuyaba@cwjamaica.com

Formerly known as Sea-Gem, if we were on a budget, this is where we would stay. Located on the beach, this very charming smallish property (22 rooms) has several cute, simple wooden gingerbread units (called Rustic Cottages), Garden Rooms (across the street), and some new, more deluxe units. The Deluxe Rooms are truly a bargain for what you pay. These rooms have terra-cotta-tiled floors, comfortable furnishings, high ceilings, and a wonderful sense of spaciousness. Kuyaba is owned by the Williams family, and managers and sons Ralph and Marc are great guys who try to use as much local wood, brick, and stone as possible when renovating units. Many of the units have air conditioning—be sure to ask, if this is necessary. They are constantly trying to make their place better for their guests. Ralph will negotiate a very fair price if you plan an extended stay.

Rates are *Cheap* (CP).

Hedonism II, P.O. Box 25, Negril Beach Road, Negril, Jamaica, W.I. Stateside and Canada: 800-467-8737. Local: 876-957-4200, fax 876-957-4289.
Web site: www.superclubs.com/brand_hedonism/

The name of this resort couldn't be more appropriate, though it's not too clear on what the "II" means (there was never a Hedonism

I, but a Hedonism III recently opened at Runaway Bay—as if another one of these places is needed!). This resort was founded on the pleasure principle and has built its reputation on sophomoric play. Personally, you'd have to pay us to stay here. This is not because we disapprove of its philosophy. It fills a valid need for many people. We simply don't find the clientele terribly sophisticated or attractive. We felt this way the first time we visited and still do over a decade later. But who needs culture and class when it comes to bodily pleasures, anyway? The management tries to sell Hedonism II with the line "Pleasure comes in many forms: the mind, the body, the spirit, and the soul." Judging from what we witnessed here, we'd say the overwhelming focus was a spirited and mindful effort to enhance the pleasures of the body to the point of selling one's soul.

The buildings and grounds are not very exciting. Frankly, the blocs of rooms look like a suburban medical center. The 280 rooms themselves are sufficient in a contemporary sense, with lots of mirrors, including one over the bed (duh!), and have a private bath and air conditioning but no balcony or patio or TV. Singles will be assigned a same-sex roommate unless they pay a single supplement. There is a rather small free-form pool that adjoins the main bar and the entertainment and dining amphitheater. The bartenders there are kept very busy, often by shouting, drunken men and women who could easily be cast in *My Cousin Vinny*, down to the gold chains around their necks and the Ozone Park accents. At the other end of the pool is the disco roof atop which is a see-through Jacuzzi (like, totally gross!). The throbbing beat of the music penetrates the poolside air. The disco bar has windows that look into the pool, much as you would find in a public aquarium. You'll see lots of dangling feet, legs, and torsos—the effect is quite provocative. There are stories of some very explicit happenings—a true exhibitionist and voyeur's dream.

Down the slope from the disco is the beach, which is nice if you want to get away from the main staging area. They have also installed a trampoline and trapeze (with safety net), for those with fantasies or fears of flying. Just about every conceivable land and water sport is available, including an ice-skating rink, a spa and fitness center, and a rock-climbing wall (clothes optional, of course). The management does pull in some superb entertainment, especially on Saturday nights. The staff, in the mode of camp counselors, is very friendly and relentlessly "up." There is also a nude pool-Jacuzzi area (open 24 hours) near the beach and at the property line (a black screen has been erected—no pun intended—to shield the neighboring buildings from probably some of the most unattractive naked bodies you'll ever be subjected to). Get the picture!?!

Rates fall into the **Beyond Belief** (All-Inclusive) range. There is a minimum two-night-stay requirement. Discounts abound most times of the year.

Montego Bay

We would avoid staying right in MoBay, as it is a city with little appeal or charm. It's crowded and hot, with traffic jams at rush hour, and bland all-inclusives along its fringes. However, just a few miles out of town are better options, including four luxury resorts that are tops on the island: Round Hill and Tryall are just west of the city, while Half Moon and a new Ritz-Carlton resort are to the east. All of these hotels have relationships with the various golf courses in the area.

Round Hill Hotel & Villas, P.O. Box 64, Montego Bay, Jamaica, W.I. Stateside: 800-972-2159. Local: 876-956-7050, fax 876-956-7505. Web site: www.roundhilljamaica.com
e-mail: roundhill@cwjamaica.com

Located 10 miles west of MoBay on a 98-acre peninsula, Round Hill is one of the grandes dames of Caribbean resorts. Since its inception in 1953, it has hosted more than its fair share of the Hollywood and jet set. There are pictures in the bar of Grace Kelly (in the buffet line) plus a score of other celebs, from Noël Coward and Queen Elizabeth to Rockefellers, Paleys, Kennedys, Andy Warhol, and Paul McCartney. This is an old-school resort, where flash is looked down upon and understatement is the name of the game. Under the continued stewardship of Josef Forstmayr, Round Hill has maintained a standard of excellence and style unparalleled in Jamaica. Occasional resident Ralph Lauren, who has owned a villa here since 1979, helped design the décor for much of the public space. His influence is apparent, especially in the bar, which would look right at home with the New York Yacht Club. There is a staff of 250 to attend to your needs; over 40 have been with Round Hill for more than 30 years—now *that*'s loyalty.

There are 28 privately owned villas (really bungalows), painted white with green trim and nestled among the hibiscus and bougainvillea. Seventeen of the villas have their own swimming pools, and all are fully staffed with maids (who cook you breakfast in your villa) and gardener. All the villas are cut up into suites (two, three, or four units each—65 in all). While each of the suites has its own entrance, this means that you will be sharing a house with someone else unless you rent the entire villa—our suggestion. Just put some friends together. That way, you won't have to share the pool or deck with anyone you don't know. Try to get villa 12—it sits on the top of the hill and has two bedrooms, a great pool, and fab views.

There are also 36 rooms in the seaside building known as the Pineapple House, affectionately called "The Barracks" since the beginning. The best rooms are on the second floor, with cathedral ceilings, large louvered windows overlooking the sea, and brightly colored walls; all are tastefully furnished. In front of "The Barracks" is a free-form pool for all guests and a small beach with water sports. Guests can play golf at Tryall for a fee.

Rates are **Ridiculous** (EP). MAP costs $80 per person per day. Villas are **Stratospheric** (includes breakfast).

The Tryall Club, P.O. Box 1206, Montego Bay, Jamaica, W.I. Stateside and Canada: 800-336-4571. Local: 876-956-5660, fax 876-956-5673.
Web site: www.tryallclub.com
e-mail: administration@tryallclub.com

Just two miles west and down the road from Round Hill, this sprawling resort is really a huge, very deluxe country club. Situated on the site of a 2,200-acre former sugar plantation and tumbling down to the sea from a far-away hilltop, this is a magnificent property, especially for those of you who love golf and tennis, the *raison d'etre* for staying at Tryall Club.

The resort itself is very grand. The U-shaped main building is an 18th-century Georgian Great House—a symphony of white, light blue, parquet and chintz. Set atop a hill, it commands expansive views of the grounds and the sea beyond. Connected to the Great House are 13 one- and two-bedroom "villa suites," all imaginatively decorated, all one-of-a-kind, and located close to the resort's restaurant, bar and main pool (the villa suites are actually a pretty good value, and come with a housekeeper-cook). Then there are 56 privately owned villas dappling the estate, and ranging from one to six bedrooms. Most of these are individually owned, and showcase the taste of the owners (most of these are pretty lavish). All have a private pool and a full-time staff (cook, chambermaid, laundress and gardener); larger villas also come with a butler. To help you decide which is right for you, the Club publishes brochures on all the villas, with photos and layouts for your perusal (also check the Web site). Down at the beach there is a beach club and watersports center, while the tennis center has nine nova-cushion courts (lit for night play), with ball machines, private lessons and clinics, and ball boys to hustle after your aberrant shots.

Rates are **Ridiculous** (EP) for rooms in the Great House, **Stratospheric** (EP) for Villas. All-inclusive plans with greens fees, some water sports, and tennis clinic are available.

Half Moon Golf, Tennis & Beach Club, P.O. Box 80, Rose Hall, Montego Bay, Jamaica, W.I. Stateside: 800-626-0592. Local: 876-953-2211, fax 876-953-2558.
Web site: web.wwide.com/halfmoon

Located six miles east of the MoBay airport, this is one of Jamaica's most deluxe resorts, and was quite popular with the Japanese market until the Asian market collapse. While not quite as chichi as Round Hill, it's just as expensive, and lots of celebrities land here (Barbara Streisand, Queen Elizabeth II, George Bush Sr., Whitney Houston for starters). The main difference with Round Hill is that this huge, 400-acre property is like a minicity, containing a shopping village (home of the Bob Marley Experience Theatre), equestrian facility and polo field, and a 24-hour medical office with dialysis center! It has a pretty, mile-long crescent beach (and other beaches on either side), a full-service spa and fitness center, 13 tennis courts for serve-and-volley enthusiasts, and four squash courts. One swimming pool is Olympic size, built for an

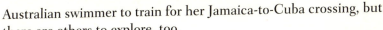

Australian swimmer to train for her Jamaica-to-Cuba crossing, but there are others to explore, too.

The main building (rebuilt in 1996 following a fire), has an antebellum-style entry replete with fountains, white columns, black and gray marble-tiles floors, crystal chandeliers, Queen Anne mahogany antiques, Oriental rugs and Jamaica art—what a combo! There are 453 rooms, which range from standard but attractive hotel rooms to four- and five-bedroom villas. The latter come with a maid, butler and live-in cook, plus a private pool.

Half Moon makes big claims about being environmentally friendly, and we're confident there's truth to the declaration. But during our last visit, we witnessed a Jamaican—albeit probably not one employed by the hotel—hauling an endangered, writhing loggerhead turtle through the surf in front of the hotel's 25-acre "nature preserve," presumably for slaughter. We pointed this out to two different security guards, who each said "he's not supposed to do that." And then they went about their chores, seemingly uninterested in trying to rescue the turtle. Having said this, Half Moon prides itself on its green program, which includes solar water heaters, organic tree mulching, and use of effective micro-organisms at the resort's sewage plant. And that's a good thing.

Rates are **Wicked Pricey** (EP), with assorted MAP, golf and all-inclusive packages also available.

The Ritz-Carlton Rose Hall, 1 Ritz-Carlton Drive, Montego Bay, Jamaica, W.I. Stateside: 800-241-3333. Local: 876-953-2800, fax 876-953-8990
Web site: www.ritzcarlton.com

A big source of local pride was the arrival of The Ritz-Carlton to Jamaica in 2000. The addition of this kind of monolith is not normally the kind of thing we applaud, but the Ritz-Carlton name is a big plus for Jamaica—it should help convince a number of Americans (the kind that need a big brand name to ensure peace of mind) to visit the island. The $125 million, 430-room Ritz-Carlton is the first "European Plan" (non-all-inclusive) resort to be built on the island since the 1970s. As such, it is a thoroughly state-of-the-art creation—even boasting its own power plant!

Located cheek-by-jowl with Half Moon, rooms are standard-issue Ritz-Carlton, with oversize sofas, framed bird and floral prints, faux antiques, and a minibar. On the downside, the five-story buildings are a bit soulless and feel hermetically sealed (to allow air conditioning in the lobby and other common areas). The man-made beach is not particularly attractive, which is probably why Ritz-Carlton also bought a beach club four miles away (the same beach, incidentally, that Richard M. Nixon proclaimed as the finest on the island—for what it's worth, Dick, we've seen better in Jamaica). On the upside, the resort debuted the island's first full-service spa, the lobby lounge has a coffee bar to serve a variety of local blends, and the impressive White Witch golf course is probably the best on the island.

Rates are **Wicked Pricey** (EP).

Wyndham Rose Hall Resort, P.O. Box 999, Montego Bay, Jamaica, W.I. Stateside: 800-WYNDHAM. Local: 876-953-2650, fax 876-953-2617.
Web site: www.wyndham.com

This 400-acre resort is best appreciated for its setting and excellent golf course (see the write-up earlier in this chapter). The hotel caters to the convention crowd, and looks it. The 489-room property was renovated in 2000, but its architecture is big, bland, pink (the company hallmark), and rectangular—none of these elements are exactly in harmony with the natural setting. Rooms are nicely decorated, but not terribly large. There is a large main pool with swim-up bar, plus an elaborate, $7 million water park with slides through a sugar mill, channels, waterfalls and faux plantation ruins, which seems to keep the children of the name-tag generation happy. For adults, there is a small shopping arcade and a casino.

Rates are **Wicked Pricey** (EP); an all-inclusive plan is available.

Coyaba Beach Resort & Club, Mahoe Bay, St. James, Jamaica, W.I. Stateside: 800-330-8272. Local: 876-953-9150, fax 876-953-2244.
Web site: www.coyabajamaica.com

Sitting on its own beach just west of Half Moon, this 50-room resort is a good spot for families with young children due to its size and various kids' programs. Owned and operated by a Jamaican family who live on site, this is a truly Jamaican enterprise and a polished one at that. All furniture has been made on the island and all produce is grown locally. Décor is island colonial style; floors are Italian tile. French doors lead out to the lanai. All kinds of water sports are available, as is a lighted tennis court. Golf is across the street.

Rates are *Very Pricey* (EP); an all-inclusive plan is available.

Ocho Rios

In past editions of *Rum & Reggae's Caribbean* we have avoided sending readers to Ocho Rios, due to its crass embrace of cruise ships and all-inclusives. But as megaboats take over an increasingly larger chunk of the Caribbean each year, and all-inclusives pepper every corner of this island, Ochi (as it's called locally) is starting to stand out less. And Jamaica Inn is a special spot, with lots of old-line appeal—you can stay here, rest-assured that you will be sequestered well away from the hustle-bustle.

Jamaica Inn, P.O. Box 1, Ocho Rios, Jamaica, W.I. Stateside: 877-470-6975. Local: 876-974-2514, fax 876-974-2449.
Web site: www.jamaicainn.com
e-mail: jaminn@cwjamaica.com

Jamaica Inn is one of the classic resorts built on the island in the 1950s that drew notables like Winston Churchill and Alistair McLean. As newer, bigger, glitzier resorts were built during the last few decades, Jamaica Inn was sometimes knocked as old fashioned or stuffy. Today, as the post–dot.com generation rediscovers glamour through the purity of a gin-clear martini, places like Jamaica Inn are back in style. Today's celebrity sightings might include I.M. Pei or Kate Moss, both of whom typify its eclectic but decidedly au courant clientele, yet all are welcomed by Eric and Peter Morrow, who grew up at the property as sons of the original owner. Ownership isn't the only thing that hasn't changed: The periwinkle blue and white color scheme remains, bullshots are served on the beach (bullion and vodka), and upon checkout guests are still presented by a handwritten bill rather than a computer printout. Some of the staff were even here at the beginning (you'll quickly recognize which ones).

A few things have evolved. The resort broke with the jacket-and-tie policy recently and has gingerly improved the property by adding things like a fitness room, and by sprucing up the rooms, but all of this has transpired without abandoning the unpretentious style of a bygone era. Every room has an ocean view, from a rise overlooking the beach. All have original tiled floors and are oversized, with large balconies stocked with sofa, wing chair, lamp and writing desk (this is a fabulous place to take in breakfast). Fabrics are cotton chintz, the four-poster beds are Jamaican antiques. There are other rooms right on the beach, plus the White Suite, where Churchill stayed—the private pool for this room has a wheelchair access ramp, built long before anyone had heard of the ADA. The pretty, covelike beach is sequestered by peninsulas on each end that keep the riff-raff out. Activities include kayaks, snorkeling equipment, tennis, and croquet. Meals are reliably good, if unelaborate, served by candlelight and accompanied by live music and dancing nightly.

Rates are **Beyond Belief** (MAP), with substantial discounts in the summer season.

Goldeneye, Orcabessa, St. Mary's, Jamaica, W.I., Stateside: 800-OUTPOST or 305-531-8800, UK: 020-7440-4360, local 876-975-3354, fax 876-975-3620
Web site: www.islandoutpost.com
e-mail: goldeneye@islandoutpost.com

We can never get enough of 007, and Goldeneye, the one-time estate of Ian Fleming, is the "birthplace" of James Bond. Thus it is semi-shrine to us. It is also the newest addition to the Island Outpost empire of Jamaica boutique hotels. If you've read through R&R properly, you know that Island Outpost runs three other Jamaican properties: Strawberry Hill, the Caves, and Jake's (and others in the Bahamas, South Beach, and Sundance, Utah). We love how owner Chris Blackwell (who started Island Records—the company that brought Bob Marley to the masses, and later U2), imparts chic style without obliterating the distinctly Jamaican ambiance of these locales. Located just east of Ocho Rios, Goldeneye includes the former home of Fleming, which is still adorned by many of the author's original furnishings—even including the desk where 14 007 novels were created. The three-bedroom home includes a high-tech media room, splendid outdoor bathtub and an elegant new pool. Original Goldeneye callers included Elizabeth

Taylor and Errol Flynn; more recent guests include Martha Stewart, Jim Carrey and Harrison Ford, most of whom have planted a tree bearing their name (Ford's original tree didn't live long, so he planted another on his second visit—the trees also signify a $1,000 donation to a local charity). Island Outpost added a cluster of four new villas on the 15-acre estate; these are beautifully decorated with batiks, outdoor tubs and handcrafted sinks. A tiny private beach is located under the rooms, and watersports are also available; nearby activities include visits to Noel Coward's home Firefly, and rafting trips on the Rio Grande. The entire property can be rented during high season for $7500/day (20% higher during the Chistmas–New Year's period (food and beverages are extra).

Rates are **Stratospheric** (EP!).

Port Antonio

Port Antonio was *the* destination for visitors in the first half of the 20th century. Made famous by movie stars like Errol Flynn (who had a villa—actually an island and plantation—here), Port Antonio today still seems stuck in the past, its glamour (and many of the resorts) faded like old color photographs. Most people today don't care about its famous past. All they want to know is if Madonna or Brad Pitt has stayed there (they haven't, but Tom Cruise filmed *Cocktail* here—whoopee!).

There aren't a helluva lot of good choices in this pretty and lush part of Jamaica. Three stand out as being well run and in good shape: Blue Lagoon, Dragon Bay, and the Mocking Bird Hill. Port Antonio is also the home of the Trident Villas and Hotel, once one of Jamaica's premier luxury destinations, which seems to be suffering from benign neglect. A German heiress has left a bizarre mark on the area with not only the creepy Jamaica Palace Hotel but also a new Bavarian-looking shopping center right in town. A few villa efficiency choices and a guest house or two round out the selection. Here we go:

Blue Lagoon Villas, Fairy Hill, P. O. Box 2, Port Antonio, Jamaica, W.I. Local: 876-993-8491, fax 876-993-8492.
Web site: www.bluelagoonvillas.com
e-mail: reservations@bluelagoonvillas.com

Port Antonio's "St. Bart's By-the-Sea," these luxurious villas are about as waterfront as you can get in Jamaica. The one-, two-, three-, and four-bedroom villas sit right on the water at the base of a lush hillside. Featured in *Vogue, Town and Country*, and more, these accommodations scream deluxe, as does the price tag. Rates start at $5,000 per week for a one-bedroom and can go well over $10,000. However, everything is included in the price. You get a car, chauffeured airport pickup, champagne on arrival, a stocked bar (Jamaican brands), air conditioning of course, maid and chef service, butler, sound system, satellite TV, tennis, access and charge account at Dragon Bay, even a helicopter landing pad. That famous Blue Lagoon is just down the street.

Rates are **Beyond Belief** (EP), including all drinks, transfers and rental car.

Dragon Bay Beach Resort, P.O. Box 176, Port Antonio, Jamaica, W.I. Local: 876-993-8751, fax 876-993-8971.
Web site: www.dragonbay.com
e-mail: reservations@dragonbay.com

If you're looking for a reasonably priced villa resort on the beach, Dragon Bay may be the one for you. Located on 55 acres along the water east of Port Antonio, this is where *Cocktail, Club Paradise*, and the remake of *Lord of the Flies* were filmed. There is a small private beach with water sports, two restaurants and a beach bar (renamed the "Cruise Bar" after you know who), and a swimming pool. Popular with Germans, the resort has a total of 107 units—a variety of rooms plus one-, two-, and three-bedroom villas—all with air conditioning and private bath. The villas come with fully equipped kitchens. Personal cooks are also available. The accommodations are comfortable and pleasantly, if simply, decorated.

Rates are **Pricey** and up (EP). Add $40 per person per day for MAP, and $85 per person per day for all-inclusive.

Hotel Mocking Bird Hill, P.O. Box 254, Port Antonio, Jamaica, W.I. Local: 876-993-7267, fax 876-993-7133.
Web site: www.hotelmockingbirdhill.com
e-mail: mockbrd@cwjamaica.com

Perched high on a hill overlooking sunsets and the coast, the ecocentric Hotel Mocking Bird Hill is set on seven acres and is the dream of two women, one Jamaican, and one Indian. Having met in Germany, Shireen and Barbara came to Jamaica and have toiled to make this 10-room inn one of the better places to stay in the Port Antonio area. Lots of thoughtful little touches, like hand-embroidered bathrobes, adorn the accommodations. The white-walled, white-tiled rooms are spacious and comfortable, with bamboo furniture, local art, ceiling fans, huge closets, safes and coffee and tea makers. Mocking Bird Hill is Green Globe Certified, which means that it meets a new international standard of environmental sensitivity for hotels and attractions.

There is a pool below the inn, and the once-pristine Frenchman's Cove beach is two miles away. A restaurant, Mille Fleurs, serves commendable Jamaican and Continental cuisine on the verandah, using local produce and seafood. Several large, friendly but barky dogs roam the premises, which can be annoying to guests (especially at dinner) and terrified our Jamaican guide. Suggestion: exclude the dogs from the common areas. There is an art gallery, Gallery Carriacou, on the premises, and the hotel welcomes people of all persuasions.

Rates are **Pricey** (EP).

Trident Villas & Hotel, P.O. Box 119, Port Antonio, Jamaica, W.I. Local: 876-993-2602, fax 876-993-2590.
Website: www.tridentvillas.com
e-mail: tridenthotel@travelpath.com

Situated just a few miles east of Port Antonio on 14 rocky waterfront acres, Trident is an institution not only in Port Antonio but also in Jamaica, having been one of its top deluxe hotels for eons. The atmosphere at Trident is decidedly British, one of quiet and reserve—very quiet, very reserved. There are no pool aerobics here. Rather, afternoon tea is served at 4:30 P.M. with sandwiches and teacakes. Croquet is set up on the lawn, and there are resident peacocks who will often fan their feathers and give you a real show (they are also quite noisy and make the strangest sounds, especially in the middle of the night). This resort is small, and staying here gives the impression of overnighting at someone's seaside estate while the owners are out of town.

There are 30 guest accommodations ranging from Superior and Deluxe rooms to Villa Suites and the grand Imperial Suite. By far the best choice is one of the wonderfully designed (if somewhat frayed) villas, which have a spacious and airy living room, private patio (except for the security guards, who will walk in front of your villa at any time—hope you're not being naughty on your patio), and a huge bedroom with lots of closet space and a large bath. There is a breakfast gazebo where room service will set up your meal and where those peacocks will sometimes entertain you (warning: don't feed them). The sound of the surf crashing against the rocks is always present.

On the grounds is a free-form pool, a small beach in a protected lagoon, and two tennis courts. The hotel has a very tasteful parlor with piano and a separate publike bar. There is a very formal dining room where the waiters wear red coats and white gloves and it feels like you can't speak above a whisper (the air conditioning and closed windows unfortunately keep out the breezes and the sound of the sea). Jackets are required. Dinner is prix fixe at $40 per person (including tip but not drinks), and the menu and food is a pleasing mix of international and Jamaican cuisine. The service is excellent, as is their special drink, the Trident Rock.

Rates are **Very Pricey** and up (MAP).

The Jamaica Palace Hotel, P.O. Box 277, Port Antonio, Jamaica, W.I. Stateside: 800-423-4095. Local: 876-993-7720, fax 876-993-7759.
Web site: www.in-site.com/jampal
e-mail: jampal@in-site.com

This is an unusual place. It looks very grand on approach, a stately and sprawling white Greek Revival building set on a hill (but not on the water). Built by a German heiress, Siglinde von Stephani-Fahmi, the Palace is geared for the European and especially the German market. A friend who was traveling with us said this place would give her nightmares. There is definitely something a tad creepy about it, *à la* the Overlook Hotel in *The Shining*. Maybe it is the eerie Baroque portrait of a woman (apparently Siglinde herself) in the lobby, or the painful-on-the-eyes black-and-white checkerboard painted concrete floors, or the asphalt-tiled pool deck that scorches your feet when you step out of the pool, or the rather odd décor in the rooms. Whatever, you get the picture.

The 80 rooms and suites are big, with high ceilings, spacious tile and marble baths, and an eclectic décor of antiques, platform beds, and chandeliers. There is a 114-foot swimming pool shaped like the island of Jamaica, and what seems like a football field of those dizzying checkerboards as a terrace (actually the roof of the building). With no shade or cover, the sun and the floor are blinding and very hot. But if the décor is not a problem, or is actually appealing, the rates are very reasonable, which may be a reason to stay here.

Rates are *Not So Cheap* and up (EP).

Goblin Hill Villas At San San, San San, Port Antonio, Jamaica, W.I. Stateside: 800-472-1148. Local: 876-925-8108, fax 876-925-6248. Web site: www.goblinhill.com
e-mail: goblinhill@n5.com.jm

This villa resort sits high up on a hill on 12 nicely landscaped acres. There are great views of San San Bay and the Caribbean from the grounds. It is peaceful and breezy, and well suited for families. There is a small pool, two lighted tennis courts, a pleasant lounge area, and the Tree Bar—a bar wrapped around the 12-foot trunk of a ficus tree.

Like most of the accommodations in the Port Antonio area, Goblin Hill could use an infusion of capital for cosmetic work, although the 28 one- and two-bedroom villas themselves are roomy and comfortable. While a '70s-looking décor prevails and may be an irritant, all villas are individually decorated; some are better than others and have large picture windows that open to the sky—a nice flourish. All have fully equipped kitchens and come with a housekeeper and cook—a definite plus. All in all a good deal.

Rates are *Not So Cheap,* including a cook/housekeeper, and airport transfers from Kingston.

Frenchman's Cove Hotel & Villas, Frenchman's Cove, Port Antonio, Jamaica, W.I. Stateside: 210-224-6868. Local: 876-933-7270, fax 876-993-8211.
Web site: www.frenchmanscove.com
e-mail: info@frenchmanscove.com

A stylish and jet-setty destination in the 1950s and '60s, Frenchman's Cove reopened in the late 1990s after having been closed for years. The results are very disappointing. What could be an awesome place to stay has, at the moment, a long, long way to go. There are 17 wonderful cut stone villas spread out along the water, all fabulously retro in design, which ache for equally fabulous furnishings and décor. If only Chris Blackwell of Island Outpost would buy and restore this property, the celebrities would pour in like a full-moon tide. At present the brown-tiled, wood-ceilinged interiors have faded wicker furniture and shabby upholstery. Air conditioners and plastic outdoor furniture are the resort's nod to the '90s. Rooms and suites are also available in the main "Great House."

Equally tragic is the exploitation of the Frenchman's Cove beach. The owner has taken one of Jamaica's prettiest beaches and opened it up to day-trippers from the big resorts of Ocho Rios and environs. They arrive in buses, are served lunch on the beach, and basically overwhelm this rather intimate cove. Guests of the hotel are the big losers here!

Rates are **Not So Cheap** for rooms and **Very Pricey** and up for villas (CP).

Bonnie View Plantation Hotel, P.O. Box 82, Port Antonio, Jamaica, W.I. Local: 876-993-2752, fax 876-993-2862.

The Bonnie View has fallen on hard times and the only thing to recommend it is the view of Port Antonio. Perched at the top of a major hill (600 feet above sea level), the views are stunning, as would be the walk down to town and back. There are 20 rundown rooms, all fan-cooled, and a restaurant and pool on the 25-acre property. Instead, come for a drink and enjoy the 360-degree panorama of Port Antonio and the Blue Mountains.

Rates are ***Cheap*** and up(EP).

DeMontevin Lodge, P.O. Box 85, Port Antonio, Jamaica, W.I. Local: 876-993-2604, no fax.

The Victoria gingerbread facade is spectacular, but almost everything else about this old guest house is shabby. Skip it unless you are on an *extremely* tight budget or want to go to dine on some good Jamaican food at the restaurant.

Rates are ***Cheap*** (EP).

The South Coast

The south coast of Jamaica is the least touristed part of the country. Partly due to a paucity of good beaches and extensive coral reefing, this region is largely ignored by most visitors to the island. However, some pockets of beauty are scheduled for mega all-inclusive development, like the pretty and lush Bluefields (there goes the neighborhood again!), but for the most part it's very unspoiled.

About 90 minutes out of Negril, or two hours from MoBay, is the tiny village of Treasure Beach. Reached through a maze of back roads where signage is virtually nonexistent, this totally local-style place with gray-sand beaches and scrubby vegetation is the home of a funky place called Jake's. A couple of days here would be refreshing from the hustle of, say, Negril.

Jake's at Treasure Beach, Calabash Bay P.A., Treasure Beach, St. Elizabeth, Jamaica, W.I. Stateside and Canada: 800-688-7678. Local: 876-965-0635, fax 876-965-0552.
Web site: www.islandoutpost.com
e-mail: jakes@cwjamaica.com

Though not for everyone, Jake's will appeal to those who want to feel far away from tourisma and like the idea of a totally barefoot and casual existence—yet in a distinctly chic setting. This is "roughing it" for the *Architectural Digest* set. Situated on a rocky coastline and about a 10-minute walk to the village beach, Jake's has some of Jamaica's most interestingly designed accommodations. Owner Sally Henzell and her son Jason have built a hodgepodge of world architectural styles to beat the band, from Jamaican and Greek to Moorish and Mexican motifs. The cottages—13 individual rooms plus two two-bedroom cottages—are all decorated with Sally's cool design sensibilities: concrete floors painted bright colors, green glass bottles embedded in the stucco walls, galvanized steel doors with punched-out designs, thatched awnings over terracotta-tiled terraces, outdoor showers, and very eclectic furnishings (colored bare-bulb lamps, for example). The best units are Seapuss (right on the water and great for romance) and the Abalone units (especially the upstairs one). All have CD-cassette players and access to an excellent CD library. Mosquito nets are provided and indeed useful (the bugs, especially sand flies, can be fierce). There is an unusual saltwater pool (which could be a tad cleaner) to refresh oneself. A myriad of activities can be arranged for you, including a trip to Y.S. Falls, crocodile viewing excursions on the Black River, mountain bike tours, and fishing excursions. Jake's restaurant serves good Jamaican cuisine. Like the place it's at, service is slow.

Rates are *Not So Cheap* and up (EP).

Kingston

If you are going to Kingston to see the Bob Marley Museum or the art scene, there are many lodging options. It's also the western end of the Jamaica–Trinidad cultural and commercial axis of the English Caribbean. By far the most spectacular and luxurious (and most expensive) accommodation is Strawberry Hill, set high up in the Blue Mountains. Although not terribly convenient to the sights and sounds of Kingston—it's about a 30-minute drive away—Strawberry Hill is a stylish place from which to sample the city rather than the big business hotels. More convenient are the big hotels, which are conveniently located in a row, are safe, and have pools in which to refresh yourself. At the properties in town, be prepared to be asked for money by small but well-rehearsed barefoot children as soon as you step off the grounds. In addition, a number of street vendors will try to sell you many things, including recorded tapes and *ganja*.

Strawberry Hill, Irish Town, Jamaica, W.I. Stateside and Canada: 800-688-7678. Local: 876-944-8400, fax 876-944-8408.
Web site: www.islandoutpost.com
e-mail: strawberryhill@islandoutpost.com

Perched at 3,100 feet in the verdant hills above Kingston and 50 minutes from the airport (for those in a hurry, there *is* a helipad), this is one of Jamaica's premier luxury hotels and the only outstanding one on the eastern half of the island. Owned by Chris Blackwell, the founder of Island Records and the man who made Bob Marley Jamaica's most famous export, Strawberry Hill is truly a magical getaway for the high-pressured, stressed, and famous. Rooms are housed in 12 Georgian-style villas that cling to the summit of the property, offering sweeping views of mountains, valleys,

Kingston, and the Caribbean. In true Island Outpost form, details which we think are *totally* key are included, like CD-cassette players and a selection of Island CDs (of course), TV-VCR on request, an intelligent library, room service, mosquito netting and heated comfortable mattresses (remember the elevation). Décor is plantation-style, with mahogany four-poster beds. All rooms have kitchenettes and private verandas with hammocks. A wonderful Aveda concept spa is on the property for that aromatic massage, and after relentless bitching by travel writers and guests alike, a fabulous 60-foot infinity pool was added.

The hotel has an excellent restaurant serving both international and Jamaican cuisine. Sunday brunch here has become an institution. There is also a cozy bar with fireplace to toss down some mean rum punches and hobnob with whomever. In keeping with the colonial thing, high tea is served in the afternoon. A roster of mountain activities including coffee plantation tours and hikes is available through the hotel.

Rates are **Wicked Pricey** and up (EP).

Le Meridien Jamaica Pegasus, P.O. Box 333, 81 Knutsford Boulevard, Kingston 5, Jamaica, W.I. Stateside: 800-543-4300. Local: 876-926-3690, fax 876-929-5855.
Web site: www.meridienjamaica.com
e-mail: jmpegasus@cwjamaica.com

With 300 rooms, this 17 floor high-rise—Kingston's tallest—sits in the middle of New Kingston, the tony area of the capital, and offers all of the amenities of an American business hotel— including 24-hour room service. Rooms are standard big-hotel fare, and each has a coffeemaker, satellite TV, radio, air conditioning (of course), safe, and a lanai. There is a large outdoor pool, two lighted tennis courts, a small health club, and a jogging track, plus two restaurants and a pub on the premises.

Rates are **Not So Cheap** (EP).

Hilton Kingston Jamaica, 77 Knutsford Boulevard, Kingston 10, Jamaica, W.I. Stateside and Canada: 800-445-8667. Local: 876-926-5430, fax 876-929-7439.

Located just north of the Jamaica Pegasus, this 303-room hotel set on over seven-plus acres is similar to the Pegasus, although we think a tad nicer. The rooms are either in the 15-story tower or in two-story wings surrounding the pool—all are pleasant and comfortable, with satellite TV, air conditioning, and a lanai. Nonsmoking floors are also available. There is 24-hour room service, an Olympic-size pool and a pool bar, floodlit tennis courts, a small health club, two restaurants, and a nightclub on the property.

Rates are *Pricey* (EP).

The Courtleigh Hotel & Suites, 85 Knutsford Boulevard, Kingston 5, Jamaica, W.I. Local: 876-929-9000, fax 876-926-7744. Website: www.courtleigh.com
e-mail: courtleigh@cwjamaica.com

Wedged between the Hilton and the Pegasus, this smaller hotel is a reasonably priced alternative to the behemoths on either side. The 78 rooms and 40 suites are furnished with four-poster beds and 18th-century mahogany reproductions. All rooms have satellite TV, air conditioning, and a safe, and nonsmoking rooms are available. There is a very small pool along with a restaurant, bar, fitness center, and business center.

Rates are *Not So Cheap* (CP).

Where to Eat

Negril

There are scores of restaurants in Negril, from small beach shacks to big hotel restaurants. Undoubtedly new ones will pop up, so be sure to ask around. But don't miss these:

Caribbean Delight, Norman Manley Boulevard, 957-4687. This is another local-style restaurant, slightly fancier than Pete's. Located just south of Negril Gardens, they serve an excellent and very cheap breakfast. $ *No credit cards.*

Chicken Lavish, West End Road, 957-4410. Simple but popular spot for tasty chicken dishes—fried, curried, etc.—plus delicious steamed fish. $

Cosmo's Seafood Restaurant and Bar, Norman Manley Boulevard, 957-4784. This is a very popular restaurant with both locals and *branché* tourists (we saw one table where everyone was wearing black—in the tropics!). It's fairly cheap and good too. Cosmos has expanded to become a restaurant-beach complex. Be sure to try the conch soup and get a T-shirt as a souvie. $$

Kuyaba, Norman Manley Boulevard, 957-4318. One of the best eateries in Negril, this on-the-beach restaurant serves superb seafood (as well as veggie, chicken, beef, and pasta) dishes with a definite Caribbean accent. Try the Cuban crab and pumpkin cakes or the coconut curried conch with mango and papaya chutney. Live music nightly. $$$

Pete's on the Beach, Norman Manley Boulevard, still no phone. Located just a little south of the Negril Gardens Hotel on the Beach, Pete's is the ultimate in *very casual* eating on the beach local-style. There are picnic tables set up about 20 feet from the water, and Pete, the chef, will grill up some mean red snapper, lobster, or chicken for you. The dj/dub music will keep your feet tapping in the sand. For dessert there is some very strong *ganja* cake—just ask for the "special cake." $

Rick's Cafe, West End Road, 957-4335. The place is totally tourist and expensive to boot, so why bother? If you must, just go at sunset and have a drink. Or try their jerk burger specials from 2 to 4 P.M. $$$ *No credit cards.*

Rockhouse, West End Road, 957-4373. A romantic, cliff-edge dining terrace and reasonable prices for classy West Indian cuisine. Make a reservation to ensure a front-row seat for Negril's famous sunset. $$

Sweet Spice, just inland, on the road to Mandeville, 957-4621. This is Negril's best institution for real Jamaican cuisine. Curried conch, oxtail in brown stew, while lobster in a variety of preparations is under $20. $$

Other places worth checking out for eats are **Peewee's** (seafood), **Fudge Pastry** (fruit cakes), **DeBuss** (jerk chicken and chips), **LTU Pub** (any and everything under the sun), **Serious Chicken** (jerk chicken), **Hungry Lion** (vegetarian/Rasta fare), **Uprising** (Jamaican cuisine), and **Erica's** (lunch).

Montego Bay

Besides eating at the above hotels, where the food ranges from very good to excellent, here are a few places in town to try:

Georgian House, 2 Orange Street, 952-0632. Probably the most elegant restaurant in Mo Bay, this is set in an old Georgian brick building in the heart of the old town. Beautiful mahogany floors and woodwork and big brass chandeliers create a very lovely, if somewhat formal, atmosphere. House specialties include tournedos Rossini, baked stuffed lobster, and pan-barbecued shrimp. Their dessert of baked bananas in coconut cream is *rich*. Reservations required. $$$$$

Julia's, Bogue Hill, 952-1772. Perched on a hill high above Mo Bay, Julia's offers Italian cuisine with an incredible view. Reservations required (they provide transportation from your hotel). $$$$

The Pelican, Gloucester Avenue, 952-3171. Jamaican cuisine, also malts and sundaes. Popular with the locals. $$$

Pork Pit, 27 Gloucester Avenue, 952-1046. Although the name is off-putting, this is a real Mo Bay institution and a must stop for anyone in the area, especially if you're driving to Negril from the airport (or returning). Jerk pork or jerk chicken is the choice, with yummy side dishes like yams and sweet potatoes. While the Pit has moved to bigger, more modern and less attractive digs (the old one had more of a parklike setting and felt like a backyard barbecue), everything is still fairly open-air and informal—you sit at tables and pig out. There are two jerk sauces, mild and hot (you can buy these to take home too). The mild will be spicy enough for most non-Jamaicans. $$ *No credit cards*

Port Antonio

The pickings here are slim. Mille Fleurs at the Hotel Mocking Bird Hill is good; dining is on the veranda. The food at the Trident is very pricey and disappointing and the atmosphere is much too formal. Your best bet is to hire a cook for the week—easily done if you have a villa. Here are a few other options:

Boston Bay Jerk Stands, Boston Bay. Right by the entrance to the beach in Boston Bay, several jerk stands, renowned throughout

Jamaica, serve the best jerk in the country. Jerk was originated in Boston Bay. Buses now arrive from Ocho Rios and other North Coast day-trips, which has jacked up the price of jerk tremendously. Be careful, it is really hot—to the point of making you cry. You can buy jars of sauce to take home. Remember, it's five-alarm stuff. $

DeMontevin Lodge Restaurant, 21 Fort George Street, 993-2604. This is probably the best Jamaican local-style restaurant in town. Specialties include pepperpot and pumpkin soup, curried lobster or chicken, and flavorful desserts. Reservations required. Very casual and cheap. $$

Dickie's Sweet Banana Shop, about a mile west of Port Antonio, just above the water on the main road; no sign, no phone. Suggested to us by our friends at Hotel Mocking Bird Hill, this is the place to come for lovely fruit and a sweet Jamaican vibe. The tiny roadside fruit shack looks at first glance like a hundred others. But Dickie, a gentle, former hotel chef turned Rastafarian, and his wife, Joy, also run a gracious and informal restaurant just behind the shack. The treehouse-like setting has room for three tables that overlook the sea. Dickie also prepares candlelight dinner by reservation (great with a full moon), though we recommend a stop for lunch when you can go for swim at the nice beach next door and enjoy the dreamy view.

Mille Fleurs, Hotel Mocking Bird Hill, 993-7267. This restaurant serves commendable Jamaican and Continental cuisine on the veranda. Chef Clarence Anderson tries to use local organic produce and seafood whenever possible. Vegetarian dishes are also featured. Reservations suggested. $$$$

Kingston

Kingston is a big city with lots of possibilities. We've selected places that are either close to the recommended hotels, as it is a big city and tourists should be alert here, or a drive or courtesy van trip away. Both the Pegasus and the Hilton have two good restaurants each, and you may be happy just to stay put. Otherwise, consider the following:

Blue Mountain Inn, Gordon Town Road, 927-1700. This is a Kingston institution, perched up in the mountains about a 15-

minute drive north of the city. The cuisine is continental/ Caribbean and the menus are changed periodically. Jackets are required for men (ties optional), but the cool night air in the mountains makes it bearable. Women should bring a wrap. This is a definite Caribbean dining experience and well worth the trip, if just for the view. Reservations are required. $$$$

Chelsea Jerk Centre, 9 Chelsea Avenue, 926-6322. For a cheap and truly Jamaican meal, namely jerk pork or chicken, within walking distance of the big hotels, this is the place. Very popular with Kingstonians. $ *No credit cards.*

Gordon's Restaurant and Lounge, 36 Trafalgar Road, 929-1390. If you're in the mood for cuisine from the Orient, Gordon's serves Chinese, Japanese, and Korean dishes. $$

Jam' Rock, 69 Knutsford Boulevard, 754-4032. It's a sports bar, it's a steak and burger joint, it's a video bar, whatever. It's always happening. $$

Hot Pot, 2 Altamont Terrace, 929-3906. A favorite for Jamaican food and fresh juices, this is a must stop for breakfast, lunch, or dinner when downtown. Ask for directions. $

Norma's on the Terrace, 26 Hope Road, Devon House, 968-5488. Owned by famed Jamaican chef Norma Shirley, once dubbed the "Julia Child of the Caribbean" by Vogue, this hot spot is located on the magnificent grounds of Devon House, a restored great house. The menu features Caribbean fusion cuisine, with Italian and French influences, like jerk chicken penne pasta or naje-poached Chilean sea bass served on cappelini and callaloo. Closed Sunday. $$$

Strawberry Hill, Irish Town, 944-8400. With views to die for, this hotel, a 30-minute drive from Kingston, has superb restaurant serving both international and Jamaican cuisine. Sunday brunch is a must. There is also a chummy bar with fireplace to rub elbows with the cognoscenti and sip a mean rum punch. Reservations required. $$$$$

Don't Miss

Overall

Ting— Jamaica's soft drink made with grapefruit juice, we just can get enough of a good Ting.
Red Stripe—It's Jamaica's beer, mon.

Negril

Miss Brown's, Sheffield Road—see description in Focus Section.
Swept Away Sports Complex—This is an excellent health club and sports center. For $25 per day, anyone (you don't have to be staying at this couples-only resort) can work out with free weights and machines, do aerobics, play squash and racquetball, play tennis on 10 courts (half of which are clay), play basketball, swim laps in a superb lap pool, take yoga classes, play pool, or take a steam or sauna. This is a great place to keep those *bis* and *tris* in tone and to work off the hangover from the previous night. Norman Manley Boulevard, 957-4040.
Y.S. Waterfall—What Dunn's River Falls used to be (that is, untouristy), Y.S. (pronounced wy-ess) is, more or less, today. Located about two-thirds of the way from Negril to Mandeville and about 10 miles north of the town of Black River, this is a good day-trip for waterfall lovers and will let you see the untrammeled part of Jamaica. The highlight for us was the jitney ride from the parking lot to the falls—you travel through pastures and vistas that are truly stunning. To get to Y.S., take the road to Savanna-la-Mar and then route A1 through Black River to Y.S. (there are signs). Open from 9:30 A.M. to 3:30 P.M. Admission is $10. Closed Mondays and holidays (there are lots of the latter, so be sure to check before going, 876-634-2454).
Margaritaville—Located on Norman Manley Boulevard in the heart of the Beach, this is daytime party central for the college and the *Real World* set (spring break is crazy here). With four open-air bars, big-screen TVs for sports and music videos, CD jukeboxes, dance floor, karaoke, beach barbecue, basketball, beach volleyball, a 30-foot water trampoline, wet T-shirt and sexy bikini contests, nightly bonfires, and live entertainment—even a

tattoo parlor—it's a mini-Daytona. There's one in MoBay too, 957-4467.

Jammin'—For live reggae or dancehall music and partying on the beach with a real mix of Jamaicans and tourists from all over, **DeBuss, Alfred's, Roots Bamboo,** and **Risky Business** alternate nights of hosting parties and shows. At press time, this was the schedule: Monday, Risky Business; Tuesday, Alfred's (recommended) and DeBuss; Wednesdays; Roots Bamboo; Thursdays, DeBuss and Risky Business; Friday, Alfred's; Saturday, Risky Business; Sunday, Alfred's and Roots Bamboo. This schedule may change, so be sure to check with your hotel or a local resident. Those who crave American dance music can head on any night to **The Jungle** a slick new club, or on Saturdays to **Compulsion** disco at #24, Plaza de Negril, although this spot is getting tired.

Pickled Parrot—With its rope swing over the water and its water slide, this West End restaurant and bar on the cliffs can be lots of fun; 957-4864.

Famous Vincent—His trips to Sandy Cay offer great snorkeling and a real character as a guide. He's a tad difficult to get hold of, but most hotels will know how to get in touch with him. Or contact Tensing Pen, 957-0357—they should know.

Jackie's on the Reef—Located on the West End, this spa offers day packages at reasonable rates that include lunch and massage. Yoga and meditation are also available. Appointments suggested; call 957-4997.

Twin Star Market—This wonderful little superette is a must stop for those staying in the West End and lacking orange juice, tonic water, even booze for their cocktails.

Rusty's X-Cellent Adventures—West End Road (near the lighthouse), 957-0155. Take a mountain bike ride with Rusty, an American who has lived in Negril for two decades. The informal tours are suitable for all abilities and take in the rural area south of the lighthouse, usually concluding at a rum shack in Little Bay.

Montego Bay

The Pork Pit—see the write-up in Where to Eat.
Margaritaville—Located on Gloucester Avenue (952-4777) and on the water right off Doctor's Cave beach, this club is a trip. Open day and night, you name it, it's here. Fifteen big-screen TVs featuring music videos and sports for the jocks among us, four open-air bars, a restaurant, CD jukeboxes, karaoke, outdoor hot tub, floating sundeck, and, the main attraction, a 110-foot water slide. There's also one in Negril. At night, a DJ spins. Free shuttles from your hotel. Cover on weekends (under $10).
Going Out—For nightlife, the hub seems to be **Margaritaville**. Also, **Pier 1** on Howard Cooke Boulevard (952-2452) is the hot spot on Fridays with a good mix of locals and tourists, **Walter's** on Gloucester Avenue (952-9391) is a sports bar and pub. **PJ's**, also on Gloucester Avenue, is a bar completely surrounded by trees, with great reggae and dancehall.

Port Antonio

Long Bay—Located about 10 miles east of Port Antonio and just a few miles east of the jerk stands at Boston Bay, this is one of the most beautiful (and undiscovered by the throngs) beaches in Jamaica. Twin mile-long crescents of uncrowded white sand, turquoise waters, and palm trees beckon. We really think this is a great place to spend the day, so you *must* stop here.
Boston Bay—There is a picturesque beach here, with small fishing boats. Try the jerk at the beach stands.
Blue Lagoon—This calm, protected cove is called the Blue Lagoon because the water is so deep (188 feet) that the water is cobalt blue. It's very scenic and fun to swim in, too. There is a dock and ladder for swimming at the Blue Lagoon Bar and Restaurant.
Rafting—Yes, Jamaica's bamboo raft rides are a touristy cliché, but they're still romantic—up there, in a way, with Venetian gondolas. In the 1950s, Errol Flynn would entice island girls aboard the two-person rafts; before that they were used to ferry bananas down to port for shipping. Today, rafts have been popularized for lovebirds, and hundreds of them ply three Jamaican rivers. The trip down the Rio Grande near Port Antonio is the classic route. Price: $45 per couple; information: 876-913-5434.

Firefly—Noel Coward's white stucco home in Port Maria, a village between Ocho Rios and Port Antonio, offers one of the most spectacular panoramas in all the Caribbean—and a history that includes visits by everyone from Queen Elizabeth to Elizabeth Taylor. Tours $12 per person; 876-725-0920

Tea at the Trident—This is fun, relaxing, and reminiscent of the glory days of the Empire. Tea is served between 4:30 and 5:30 P.M. After tea, have a Trident Rock, their special drink; 993-2602.

Kingston

Port Royal—A 30-minute ferry ride will take you to this former "wickedest city on earth," located at the end of the airport peninsula, which was mostly swallowed up by the sea in the 1692 earthquake. The ferry ride is $1 round-trip and it departs Kingston five times daily starting at 10 A.M.

Lime Cay—Kingston's best beach is on an islet off of Port Royal and is a fun boat excursion. Avoid on weekends!

Bob Marley Museum—see write-up at beginning of this chapter.

The National Gallery—see write-up at beginning of this chapter.

INDEX

Art Gallery Ltd., 16
art, 14-16, 33

bars and clubs, 45-46
before you go, xvii
best beaches, xxi-xxii
Bloody Bay, xxi
Blue Lagoon Villas, 31
Blue Lagoon, 47
Blue Mountain Inn, 43
Bluefields Bay, xxii
Bob Marley, 13-14
Bob Marley Museum, 13, 48
Bolivar Bookshop & Gallery, 15
Bonnie View Plantation Hotel, 36
Boston Bay, xxii, 47
Boston Bay Jerk Stands, 42

Caribbean Delight, 40
Catcha Falling Star, 19
casino, 28
Caves, The, 19
Chelsea Art Gallery, 16
Chelsea Jerk Centre, 44
Chicken Lavish, 40
climate, xvii
Contemporary Arts Centre, 15
Cosmo's Seafood Restaurant, 40
Courtleigh Hotel & Suites, The, 40
Coyaba Beach Resort, 28

dancing, 10, 23, 45-46
DeBuss, 41
Demontevin Lodge Restaurant, 43
DeMontevin Lodge, 36
Dickie's Sweet Banana Shop, 43
Don't Miss, 45
Dragon Bay Beach Resort, 32

Edna Manley School, 15
Erica's, 41

Famous Vincent, 46
favorites, xx-xxii
Firefly, 48
Frame Centre Gallery, 16
Frenchman's Cove Hotel, xxi, 35
Fudge Pastry, 41

Georgian House, 42
getting around, 7
getting there, 6
Goblin Hill Villas, 35
Goldeneye, 30
golf, 16-17, 25-26, 26-27, 28, 29
Gordon's Restaurant and Lounge, 44
Greens by the Sea, 16

Half Moon Beach Club, 17, 26
health club and spas, 20, 26, 45, 39, 40
Hedonism II, 22
Hilton Kingston Jamaica, 39
history, 4
Hot Pot, 44
Hotel Mocking Bird Hill, 32
Hungry Lion, 41

Institute of Jamaica, 16
Ironshore, 17

Jackie's on the Reef, 46
Jake's at Treasure Beach, 37
Jam' Rock, 44
Jamaica Inn, 29
Jamaica Palace Hotel, The, 34
Jamaican art, 14
Jammin, 46
Julia's, 42

INDEX

key facts, 6
Kingston, 38-40, 43-44
Kuyaba, 41
Kuyaba Resort, 22

Le Meridien Jamaica Pegasus, 39
Lime Cay, xxii, 48
Long Bay, xxi, 47
LTU Pub, 41

map, viii-ix
Margaritaville, 45, 47
Mille Fleurs, 43
Miss Brown's, 45
Montego Bay, 16, 24-29, 42
music, reggae, 11-14
Mutual Life Gallery, 16

National Gallery, 15, 48
natural sites, waterfalls, 45
Negril, 9-11, 18-21, 40-41
Negril Beach, xxi
Negril Cabins Resort, 21
nightlife, 46, 47
Norma's on the Terrace, 44
nude beaches, 19, 21

Ocho Rios, 29-31
overview, 1

packing, xix-xx
Peewee's, 41
Pelican, The, 42
Pete's on the Beach, 41
Pickled Parrot, 46
Pier 1, 47
PJ's, 47
Pork Pit, 42, 47
Port Antonio, 31-36, 42-43
Port Royal, 48

rafting, 47
Red Stripe, 45
reggae, 11-13

Reggae Sumfest, 14
resorts & hotels, 18-40
restaurants, 40-44
Rick's Café, 41
Ritz-Carlton Rose Hall, The, 27
Rockhouse, 20, 41
Round Hill Hotel, 24
Rum & Reggae Punch, xxv
Rusty's X-Cellent Adventures, 46

San San, xxii
Sandy Bay, xxii
Serious Chicken, 41
Seven Mile Beach, 21-24
snorkeling, 46
south coast, 37-38
Strawberry Hill, 38, 44
Sweet Spice, 41
Swept Away Sports Complex, 45

tanning, xviii
tea at the Trident, 48
tennis, 25, 26, 29, 32
Tensing Pen, 18
things to do, 14-16, 17, 45-48,
Ting, 45
touristo scale, xxiv
transportation, 6-7
Treasure Beach, xxii
Trident Villas & Hotel, 33
Tryall Club, The, 16, 25
Twin Star Market, 46

Uprising, 41

Walter's, 47
water sports, 23, 25, 28
waterfalls, 45
what to wear, xviii-xx
White Sands, 21
White Witch, 28
Wyndham Rose Hall, 17, 28

Y.S, Waterfall, 45

Write to Rum & Reggae

Dear *Rum & Reggae Jamaica* Readers,

We really do appreciate and value your comments, suggestions, or information about anything new or exciting in the Caribbean. We'd love to hear about your experiences, good and bad, while you were in the tropics. Your feedback helps us shape the next edition. So please let us hear from you. Here's how:

Visit our Web site at: www.rumreggae.com
e-mail us at yahmon@rumreggae.com
or write to:

Mr. Yah Mon
Rum & Reggae Guidebooks
P.O. Box 152
Prides Crossing, MA 01965

Sincerely,
Jonathan Runge

P.S.—We often mention cocktails, drinking, and other things in this book. We certainly do not mean to offend any nondrinkers or those in recovery. Please don't take offense--rum and its relatives are not a requirement for a successful vacation in the Caribbean.

The Author

JONATHAN RUNGE is the author of ten other travel books: *Rum & Reggae's Caribbean* (2002), *Rum & Reggae's Puerto Rico* (2002), *Rum & Reggae's Dominican Republic* (2002), *Rum & Reggae's Cuba* (2002), *Rum & Reggae's Hawai'i* (2001), *Rum & Reggae's Caribbean 2000*, *Rum & Reggae's Caribbean: The Insider's Guide to the Caribbean* (1993); *Hot on Hawai'i, The Definitive Guide to the Aloha State* (1989); *Rum & Reggae, What's Hot and What's Not in the Caribbean* (1988); and *Ski Party! The Skier's Guide to the Good Life*, co-authored with Steve Deschenes (1985). Jonathan has written for *Men's Journal, Outside, National Geographic Traveler, Out, Skiing, Boston,* and other magazines. Future books to be published in 2002 from Jonathan Runge include *Rum & Reggae's Brasil*.